MASTERS AT WORK

MASTERS AT WORK

BECOMING AN ETHICAL HACKER

GARY RIVLIN

SIMON & SCHUSTER

New York   London   Toronto   Sydney   New Delhi

Simon & Schuster
1230 Avenue of the Americas
New York, NY 10020

First Simon & Schuster hardcover edition May 2019

SIMON & SCHUSTER and colophon are registered
trademarks of Simon & Schuster, Inc.

For information about special discounts for bulk purchases,
please contact Simon & Schuster Special Sales at 1-866-506-1949
or business@simonandschuster.com.

The Simon & Schuster Speakers Bureau can bring authors to
your live event. For more information or to book an event, contact
the Simon & Schuster Speakers Bureau at 1-866-248-3049
or visit our website at www.simonspeakers.com.

Manufactured in the United States of America

1   3   5   7   9   10   8   6   4   2

Library of Congress Cataloging-in-Publication Data is available.

ISBN 978-1-5011-6791-1
ISBN 978-1-5011-6792-8 (ebook)

To my mother, Naomi Rivlin, with love

CONTENTS

PROLOGUE

Angela Gunn is fried. This is one of those frantic periods when it feels as if she works in an ER or at a fire station rather than holding a staff position with a computer security firm. It's just after Labor Day 2018, and she's chosen as our meeting place a café with a dive-bar vibe in a trendy stretch of Seattle's downtown. Called Bedlam, Gunn declared the place "thematically appropriate" for any discussion that involves her life and job. A frazzled Gunn plops down in a seat across from mine. "I'm a hot mess today," she declares.

This is her life every August, Gunn explains. Invariably, it's the same around Christmas and New Year's as well. She's busiest when the rest of the world is on vacation and online fraud peaks. "People attack when they think your guard is down," Gunn says. At the time of my visit, she was juggling three cases. That made for a hectic August that spilled into September. All three were coming to a close, but she had been roped into a fourth. "I was up till four a.m. last night and it wasn't even one of my cases," she says. The late hours were because she needed to speak with the firm's malware—malicious software—specialist, who lives in Australia. "A brilliant guy. I respect the hell out of him," Gunn says. "I just wish he didn't live nineteen time zones away." Her job over the next twenty-four to forty-eight hours will be to find the people her firm needs for this latest case. "My guy can't get here so I need to find boots on the ground," she says. "So now it's about making alliances with people known for wearing hats that are some shade of white."

Gunn orders a tall Rose Mocha latte that the menu describes with flowery prose: "Imagine walking in a garden, cool and in the bright sun, a fountain splashing softly, the faint sweet scent of roses & chocolate full of Eastern promise." After reading it out loud to me, Gunn starts rattling off jokes about the new Seattle (she first moved to the city in the late 1990s) and for good measure takes a couple of biting digs at Amazon, which she and others I meet with while in town cast as an Evil Empire, practically swallowing whole the city they love. She brightens when her Rose Mocha arrives. It's been a rough few weeks, Gunn tells me, "I could use a cool walk through a garden right about now."

It's people like Gunn that organizations large and small call if they've had a data breach or suspect they have. People in the industry—cybersecurity, if you'd like, though Gunn's preference is information security, or "info-sec" for short—call this "incident response." To my mind, though, they're the online world's firefighters: those who rush to put out the flames and then assess the damage. Ten years ago, Gunn was working as a tech journalist. Now she works full-time for a long-standing British security firm called BAE Systems, which hired her a couple of years earlier to help them establish a presence in Seattle. Her title is "incident response consultant," and it's her job to assemble the small crew she needs for each case. Typically, that includes an analyst who can pore over computer logs, a malware specialist, and those she dubs "forensic workers, except without the formaldehyde smell and ripped-open chest cavities." That's if she can find any live bodies to do the work.

"Right now, I'd sell a right toe for a forensics guy," Gunn says. "Like a lot of people in info-sec right now, we're agonizingly understaffed."

That morning she had been on the University of Washington campus for the quarterly gathering of the Seattle-area computer security group to which she belongs. As usual, that day's talk, about the special precautions a security team must take to protect power grids, water treatment centers, and other critical infrastructure, was off-the-record. The idea, she explains, is to create a safe space for people so they can speak freely without fear of the consequences. "It's a network of trust. Except when it comes to stealing everyone's best people," she says. People don't say hello so much as let one another know what postings they have that remain open. "A typical conversation goes, 'Oh my God, where did you land?' They'll say Amazon and you ask, 'Oooo, are you okay?'" Gunn has been in the business for eight years—if not quite an old hand, then someone who has learned a lot since taking a job at Microsoft, in 2010, where she helped manage the company's message to the wider world when a bug hit Windows or another Microsoft product.

"People in security are changing jobs it seems every year, if not every six months," Gunn says. "At the meeting just now, I was like, 'Maybe one of you guys is my next analyst.' Except they're hoping I'll join their team." A 2015 report by the job analytics firm Burning Glass Technologies found that postings for cybersecurity had grown more than three times faster than other information technology (IT) positions, and roughly twelve times faster than all other jobs. The firm also reported that those working cybersecurity on average earn nearly 10 percent more than others in IT.*

IT WASN'T THAT LONG ago that computer security was more of a niche job category—a wise career choice, perhaps, but a specialty that relegated an employee to a backwater of the computing world. The release of the 1983 movie *WarGames* woke up many to the importance of cyber-security in a digital age, including then president Ronald Reagan, who saw the movie the day after its release. Reagan was among those frightened by its depiction of Matthew Broderick as a teen tech whiz who unwittingly breaks into a military computer and nearly triggers World War III. Fifteen months later, in September 1984, the National

---

* "Job Market Intelligence: Cybersecurity Jobs, 2015," Burning Glass Technologies, https://www.burning-glass.com/wp-content/uploads/Cyber security_Jobs_Report_2015.pdf.

Security Agency, or NSA, released a policy directive dryly titled, "National Policy on Telecommunications and Automated Information Systems Security." The generals and spy chiefs around Reagan concluded that the film wasn't as far-fetched as they might have hoped. The government's systems, the policy directive said, were "highly susceptible" to attack by foreign powers, terrorist groups, and criminals. Yet networking was still an esoteric issue then, even among computer scientists, and personal computers were only starting to appear inside corporate America and in people's homes. Most people working info-sec then toiled in the bowels of the Pentagon or worked for a big defense contractor.

Slowly, the rest of the world woke up to cybersecurity and the importance of protecting computers, networks, applications, and data from unauthorized access. The invention in the late 1980s of the "World Wide Web" helped to popularize the internet throughout the 1990s (the web is a user-friendly interface built on top of the internet). But the move online brought with it worms, viruses, and malware. Commerce came to the internet, along with thieves and scammers. We bought security software packages from companies such as

McAfee and Symantec, but then used passwords often no more sophisticated than 12345 or a spouse's name. People talked about computer security but it still wasn't something most colleges taught. The spread of wireless network—Wi-Fi—made it easy for us to connect our laptops, including work laptops, to the open networks in cafés, airports, and libraries, potentially exposing our personal information to those tech savvy enough to hack into a network. Wi-Fi also inspired "wardriving"—people creeping along in a car, searching for un-secure networks to infiltrate, maybe for the fun of it, maybe for more nefarious reasons—which, eventually, schooled us on the importance of a secure network.

The advent of thumb drives—USB memory sticks—proved an easy way to transfer documents from one computer to another but also an efficient way to infect a machine with malware. The nanny cams and other gizmos we linked to our networks posed another threat, punching holes in our firewalls and offering potential back doors into our private lives. "All these consumer-grade devices are made as cheaply as possible," said Mark Seiden, who has been working in computer security since the 1990s. "They use old, unpatched software and a lot of it isn't even upgradeable." Our smartphones and the tablets we've connected to our networks tend to have better security than these cheap, more disposable items, but there's the so-called Internet of Things, which is this idea that cheap computer chips will be added to everyday items, including the internet-connected devices that transform the places we live into a "smart home": smart locks on our front doors and smart thermostats and smart lights, all connected to the same Wi-Fi networks we use to do our banking and carry on private conversations. And now, of course, there are the listening devices people have welcomed into their homes in the form of the voice-activated assistants sitting on the kitchen counters of tens of millions of Americans. Is it any wonder that old hands like Seiden speak of an "attacker's advantage"? "You're a business that does everything right but an employee installs a device on the network which has a vulnerability and it opens you up," Seiden said. He should know: for years he has jobbed himself out to big companies looking for help testing their defenses. "With everything we're connecting to our networks, there's definitely an attacker advantage today," Seiden noted. Cybercrime caused an estimated $3 trillion in damages in 2015, according to the research firm

Cybersecurity Ventures. It expects that figure to double to $6 trillion by 2021.*

We survived phishing scams and browser popups and the danger when opening attachments from unknown senders and hijacked Facebook accounts. Yet we now have ransomware. Risk being exposed in front of your friends, spouse, or employer unless the victim sends bitcoin to the hackers who intercepted something incriminating or embarrassing. Or the hostage could be the user's system. The victim must spend a small fortune cleaning up the malware some no-goodniks have slipped onto their server— or pay the ransom and get back to business. Victims of this second type of attack have included Fortune 500 companies, hospitals, and even police departments. Our financial lives exist online, along with our photos, texts, and medical records. Corporations store their most precious secrets in the cloud, along with ours, including our credit card numbers, social security numbers, and passwords. Yet for more than a decade, we've been reading about the huge data breaches hitting one big company after another, including

---

* Steven Morgan, "Cybercrime Damages $6 Trillion by 2021," Cybersecurity Ventures, October 16, 2017, https://cybersecurityventures.com /hackerpocalypse-cybercrime-report-2016/.

Uber, Google, eBay, and Equifax. Reported data breaches in the United States hit a high of more than 1,500 in 2017—a jump of nearly 45 percent over the previous year.* Among those hit in 2018: Facebook, where flaws in its code gave hackers access to fifty million accounts, including those of Mark Zuckerberg and his nearly-as-famous number two, Sheryl Sandberg.

"Our power grid, our cars, our everyday devices— basically everything is online and able to be attacked," Georgia Weidman, the author of *Penetration Testing: A Hands-On Introduction to Hacking*, told the *New York Times* in 2018. Our water supply is increasingly digitized, and therefore more vulnerable to attack. So, too, are the world's dams if a malicious hacker "decided to open all their sluices. That's actually something that could happen," Weidman said. There will always be "black hats"—those looking for vulnerabilities in a computer system or network to do harm. Sometimes black hats are state-sponsored operatives who steal private data and disrupt or shutdown websites and networks. More often they're small-time hustlers

* "2017 Annual Data Breach Year-End Review," Identity Theft Resource Center, https://www.idtheftcenter.org/2017-data-breaches/.

seeking credit card information or bank account numbers and passwords. A corollary to Mark Seiden's "attacker's advantage" is the "defender's dilemma," which Dave Weinstein, a security manager inside Google, summed up this way: "The defender has to be strong everywhere, every day. The attacker only has to win once." For each set of bad guys, there needs to be veritable armies on the defense side, beefing up armaments and rushing to the rescue at the first sign of an attack.

The march of technology, in other words, has created a huge demand for ethical hackers, or "white hats": those skilled at using computers who can protect our systems and battle those with bad intentions. By now any university offering a computer science degree invariably offers classes in security. The more forward-looking among them have created a dedicated Computer Security department and offer a bachelor's degree in cybersecurity. Still, businesses are having a hard time finding people to work computer security. At the end of 2018, for instance, there were more than twenty-six thousand openings for a "cybersecurity analyst" (average pay: $85,000 a year), according to CyberSeek, which is part of a program nested under the U.S. Department of Commerce. An "incident analyst/

responder," though an entry-level position, paid an average of $99,000, yet the CyberSeek career survey found 6,600 openings. Senior positions, of course, pay more: $129,000 for a "cybersecurity architect," for instance, or a lot more if working at a place like Google or Microsoft. "If someone has six months to a year of work and, when they came in for an interview, they didn't pee on the rug, they're going to make in the neighborhood of $85,000," Angela Gunn said. "If they have a special skill—if they have experience doing database scanning or maybe they worked as a programmer before moving to security—then they're going up to 110, 120, 125." For those with five or more years of experience, she said, the salaries start at $150,000. "There was never a cybersecurity job that I took where I was like, 'Man, I wish I could make more money,'" said Billy Rios, who worked for Microsoft and then Google before venturing off on his own.

All told, according to CyberSeek, just over 700,000 people were working cybersecurity for U.S.-based businesses and other organizations in 2018, not including 300,000-plus unfilled positions. How crazy is the demand for quality people in info-sec? A security reporter I know was wearing a free T-shirt he had picked up at an industry event while waiting for a table at a San Francisco restaurant. A stranger struck up a conversation: "My company is hiring security people. You have a résumé?" The on-the-spot recruiter worked for Square, a publicly traded mobile payments company worth in the tens of billions. "You'll greet someone you know in the information security space," Google's Dave Weinstein said, "and say, 'Hey, how's it going, we're hiring!' And the other person says, 'Oh, we're hiring too!' Only then can you move on with your conversation." The data point that had people inside the cybersecurity world buzzing in 2017 was a prediction by Cybersecurity Ventures that by 2021, there will be roughly 3.5 million unfilled cybersecurity jobs across the globe.[*]

It's those on the defense side of things—those working to protect and defend our apps, data, devices, and networks from cyberattacks—who are the subject of this book: good-guy ethical hackers, though the word *hacker* is so loaded that it demands to be defined. Within these pages, it's a neutral term used to describe any super-programmer with a gift for outwitting computer systems, often by weaknesses in the existing code. That includes those with bad intentions

---

[*] Steven Morgan, "Cybersecurity Jobs Report 2018-2021," Cybersecurity Ventures, May 31, 2017, https://cybersecurityventures.com/jobs/.

who manage to get inside a seemingly well-fortified system but also those on the defense side of things. The Russian operatives who broke into the Democratic National Committee's servers and stole its e-mails are hackers but so are those in the business of sniffing out and preventing such attacks. Consider the term *life hack*. A life hack can be a cheat but more often it's a clever fix to an everyday activity.

Those I spoke with tend to use white hats and black as shorthands to distinguish between hackers with good intentions and those seeking to do harm. But even there you dare an argument. A definition I heard that I liked is that if you're interested in a computer bug to fix a problem, you're wearing a white hat; if you're interested in that bug because you want to use it, you're wearing a black hat. But what about when the U.S. government infected an Iranian nuclear facility with the Stuxnet worm? "Is that ethical or not?" asked Dave Weinstein. "It represented a significant setback to a nuclear program, which is a distinctly safer alternative than a large-scale nuclear strike, which was one of the options on the table." Yet Stuxnet also seems textbook black hat: deliberately harming a machine by infecting it with a particular noxious form of malware. Or what about Captain Crunch, a former U.S. Air Force radar technician and early hacker who discovered in the late 1960s that the toy whistle that came in boxes of Cap'n Crunch could be used to make free long-distance calls (the 2600-hertz tone it emitted was the same frequency used by one of the big long-distance networks). He was in effect using technology to steal, but was he a black hat? The ambiguities of examples like these help explain another term people throw around: "gray hats." I've grown to prefer "ethical hacker," which I picked up talking with those in info-sec.

The world's internet service providers (ISPs), wireless carriers, and others in the network business are always looking for good security people, as are all the big tech companies, including Google, Microsoft, and Amazon. While testifying before Congress in spring 2018, Mark Zuckerberg promised to add ten thousand employees to its ranks to handle cybersecurity and content management to protect user data. These days, every big tech company has multiple offices around the globe, meaning a person can get a computer security job with Cisco in San Jose, where the company has its headquarters, or outside Baltimore, where its Talos threat intelligence and research group is based, or Austin, Texas, where Talos operates a satellite office. Banks need small battalions of IT security people in its offices around the globe, as do health-care companies, retailers, and pretty much any business whose chief executives live in fear of a data breach that brings unwanted media attention. So, too, do governments and nonprofits and universities as well as small and medium-sized businesses. Those that can't afford a dedicated cybersecurity team (and even some that can) have contracts with consultancies and other businesses that help them build and maintain their defenses.

The job options themselves are varied and allow for different skill levels and personalities. "What's great about computer security is the range," Mark Seiden said. For those seeking a more traditional work schedule, there are ample jobs in auditing and compliance. These are the legions that businesses hire to ensure that its people are following its own rules and procedures and those imposed by any relevant regulatory agencies. These are the "clerks and accountants" of the info-sec world, Seiden said, who can be found working for the companies themselves or at tech consulting firms or the country's accounting giants, which are among those that have moved into cybersecurity. "It's not particularly fascinating work, but it's the kind of job that'll let you raise a family and work regular hours and make a good salary,"

Seiden continued. There are also the insurance adjustors who investigate the claims for businesses carrying the cyber insurance that compensates them in case they're the victim of a data breach or other cybercrimes. There are also policy jobs to be had inside government and businesses. These are the people who write the rules and protocols that everyone must follow when handling people's personal data.

Management jobs are plentiful: database administrator, cybersecurity administrator, auditing chief. The bigger tech companies like Google and Microsoft have layers of managers among its security people (a couple of whom you'll meet here). Sitting atop the corporate org chart is increasingly a new addition to the executive suite: chief security officer (CSO), or chief information security officer (the CISO, or "sea-so"). A new set of privacy protections implemented by the European Union in 2018 has given rise to another new executive position: the Data Protection Officer (DPO).* Yet, of course, the higher one ascends the corporate ladder, the more vulnerable that person might

---

* Nate Lord, "What Is a Data Protection Officer (DPO)? Learn About the New Role Required for GDPR Compliance in 2019," Data Insider, January 23, 2019, https://digitalguardian.com/blog/what-data-protection-officer-dpo-learn-about-new-role-required-gdpr-compliance.

find him- or herself. "Being an IT security manager is a job fated to failure," Seiden noted. Eventually, some kind of incident is going to happen. One bad breach and, like the manager or coach of a sports team, the person overseeing security plays the fall guy: fired because management needs to do *something* in response.

Those like Seiden, who does penetration testing ("pen testers" if speaking like an insider), are an interesting breed. These are the operatives businesses hire to test their defenses in the hopes they discover any weaknesses in their systems before they're exploited by a real attack. "Twisting doorknobs for a living," as Seiden described it, which could mean virtual entranceways or real ones. Billy Rios, an ex-marine good with computers, landed a job in his midtwenties with Ernst & Young, which had recently formed a pen-testing crew it was jobbing out to large corporations. "We were kicking doors in, picking locks, hiding in closets and bathrooms, stuff like that. It was great fun," Rios said. That part of the job is what people in the business call "physical security." The best pen testers are good at both.

Those called "security researchers" also search for vulnerabilities, though in their case no one is hiring them to do so. These "bug hunters" are at once the elites of the info-sec universe and occupy a more ambiguous perch. A St. Louis man with whom I spoke, Charlie Miller, described himself as a "good-guy hacker." Yet Miller was also the first person to hack the iPhone. He's also broken into an Android phone, a MacBook and, with a friend, commandeered a moving Jeep Cherokee (including its steering wheel, brakes, and accelerator) via the car's built-in cellular connection. The Jeep he hacked into was his own, as were all the other devices he exploited. In each case, he let the target companies (Apple, Google, Chrysler) know months in advance of going public with a vulnerability, so as to give them time to fix the problem. "I'd describe myself as a white hat but a lot of people say we're gray hats because we find these vulnerabilities and publicize them," he said. After stints at Ernst & Young, Microsoft, and Google, Billy Rios would join the ranks of security researchers. He and his partners probe for holes in medical devices—and have found them in such essential instruments as insulin pumps and heart regulators. The device makers may view him as a pest, if not worse, but he sees himself as potentially helping to save lives. "It almost feels sterile when you're giving the presentation to a group of hackers but then someone goes, 'What can you do with this?' And I'm like, 'Dude, you can kill someone,'" Rios said.

Security researcher is the glamour position of the info-sec world. You see them quoted in *Wired* and the *New York Times* and find them onstage at conferences. There are two premier hacker events each year, Black Hat and DEF CON, or three if you include RSA, which is an industry trade show that draws some of the same big-name speakers. Black Hat and DEF CON are held back-to-back in Las Vegas every summer. Black Hat drew over seventeen thousand people when it celebrated its twentieth anniversary in 2017, and DEF CON, which is a few years older, attracted more than thirty thousand participants. Black Hat, despite what its name might imply, is the more corporate of the two conferences; it's DEF CON that is geared more toward hackers and hobbyists and is focused more on breaking things and mischief. A commonly voiced adage about the two conferences: Black Hat is the university and DEF CON the fraternity. "Black Hat tends to focus on new attacks with the goal of promoting awareness of a vulnerability, so that users can protect themselves and technology developers can start thinking about how to implement fixes," said Harvard computer science professor James Mickens. By contrast, Mickens continued, DEF CON is known as "the funner, more interesting conference that has more of a maker community feel, with capture-the-flag competitions, tutorials on lock picking, and the like." Maybe it was just as well that Black Hat 2018 is where Rios and his partner, Jonathan Butts, exposed the latest vulnerability they had found in a medical device—a pacemaker. "We were going to get a veterinarian to implant a pacemaker in a pig to show people that this is for real," Rios said. "The Black Hat folks kind of walked us off the bridge on that one."

And then there's Angela Gunn's world of incident response, which offers any number of pathways into info-sec. Gunn described herself as "technical but not as technical as my tech guy." But then her "tech lead," she said, "isn't as technical as his deep-dive guys." These include the "log analysts" and "host analysts" who are doing more root directory work. "These are people who look at the traffic coming or going, or are trying to figure out why the system did what it did," she said. "And out on the fringes we have the malware guy. Just slide a pizza under the door and don't talk to him and he'll be happy." Her favorites seem those she dubs the "malware hunters," who study the beasts once they are trapped in what info-sec people sometimes call "the sandbox"—a safe space where a virus can't do additional damage. "There are certain engineers who want to be that guy who opens up that malware and sees its beating heart," Gunn said. That's the Australian engineer she had been talking to in the middle of the night. "You can tell it feeds his soul," she said. "You can tell he found his place."

That is essentially true of all the people you'll meet here: Each seems to have found his or her proper place in the world with work that gives life meaning and helps feed his or her soul. Gunn is the focus of the first chapter: someone happy to the extent that is possible in a stressful, intense job that occasionally causes her to reach a breaking point. The focus of chapter two is Mark Seiden, an impish computer prodigy with the pluck of a con man—in the parlance of information security, a master of social engineering (here, eliciting information from people through deception). These days Seiden, who is in his sixties, takes on all kinds of projects, but in his day he was a master pen tester, as good as any in the business at sniffing out creases in the security systems of some of the planet's largest corporations. He might slip on a FedEx shirt and push a hand truck for a caper, or play the part of the Iron Mountain employee there to pick up boxes of sensitive information bound for the shredder. "It's amazing what a windbreaker and clipboard can do," said Seiden, a former IBM programmer who also worked for the legendary Xerox PARC.

Parisa Tabriz and Dave Weinstein are the focus of two chapters: ministers of defense, as I see them, occupying important jobs at Google. Weinstein is a middle manager doing security for Android, the operating system the company wrote for mobile devices—no easy job given how often Android is in the news because of a security breach. (A sample headline from 2018: "Here we go again: Newly discovered Android vulnerability can be used to spy on you.") Tabriz is the self-proclaimed "security princess" who oversees Chrome, the globe's dominant web browser. She is the more acclaimed of the two—and, as a director of engineering at Google, much higher on the company org chart. Tabriz has been on CNN and profiled in *Elle* and *Wired*, which in 2017 put her on its list of "20 Tech Visionaries." She has lectured at Harvard's Kennedy School and consulted both with the White House during Barack Obama's presidency and with Hollywood writers interested in a more accurate depiction of cybersecurity in movies and on TV. Maybe most impressively, she was the keynote speaker at Black Hat in 2018.

Patrick Wardle, one of the more interesting bug hunters

I came across, is the focus of the next chapter. Wardle, who went from emancipated minor at age fifteen to a hilltop in Maui, worked at the NSA, the U.S. government's main spy agency, before venturing out on his own. He is not yet thirty-five, but has already cofounded a pair of startups. He also might stand as Apple's least favorite person in the security world. The best way to make a name for yourself in the security research world is to have a specialty. "You really want to be an expert in one thing," Wardle said—he chose macOS.

Finally, there's Allison Wong, whose story I tell because hers is one that demands to be told. A working-class kid from Houston, her introduction to the internet was the PC her family kept in the living room so they could stay in touch with her father, who was in the military. She was programming by age ten; by fifteen, she was working tech support at a local ISP, less for the money, she said, than the free bandwidth. She was seventeen when she went to work at NASA on the space shuttle program. By twenty-one, she was a globetrotting security consultant and engaged to a Ukrainian hacker.

Now thirty-eight, Wong has done a little bit of everything in the computer security world. She spent several years as a firefighter and has done her share of penetration testing. She's also done defense work for major companies including eBay and Visa, and created products for McAfee and Symantec. These days she is the CEO of the security startup she cofounded with a friend, and active in Women in Technology, a group that reaches into area high schools and local colleges to get girls thinking about the potential for a career in science, technology, engineering, or math (STEM).

It's never more obvious how great a life in computer security can be, Wong said, as when she speaks before an auditorium of young women. "The idea is to get girls to look at computers as a career path," she said. "I always say the same thing at these things," Wong told me: At least consider info-sec as a career path. It's a sector that offers a wide range of options and the pay is a huge plus. "It's a cool job," she'll say. "If you stay in it for four years and show you're good, you'll make in the six figures. And not just the low six figures." Plus one more advantage, she tells them. "It's not a job you can get bored at. If you get bored, you're doing something wrong."

1

FIREFIGHTERS

Some are born geeks. The only question is whether they'll end up in cybersecurity or doing some other aspect of computer work. Craig Williams, for instance, was in kindergarten and playing on an old Apple computer when he discovered that by clicking on the control panel icon, he could change the display colors on a screen, thereby messing with teachers who had no clue what had happened. "I've known exactly what I wanted to do pretty much for my entire life," said Williams. Today, Williams is thirty-eight years old and handsomely paid as a manager for an elite security team inside Cisco. By comparison, Allison Wong was a late bloomer: not until she was around eight did she first touch one of the machines that would change her life.

Angela Gunn, by contrast, didn't discover info-sec as a career until she was on the wrong side of forty. Gunn, who had grown up in a small town in Nebraska, had studied philosophy at Occidental College, a small liberal arts college in Los Angeles. She thought she might want to write about architecture until learning, she said, "there's very little money in that." She figured she had scored big when she secured an interview with a new literary magazine called *Wigwag* that had been started by a group of exiles from *The New Yorker*, "but it closed before I even got to New York." She would become a de facto tech journalist, not from any deep affinity for computers but "because that's where the jobs were in the early 1990s." She took a job at *PC Magazine*, where she quickly moved up the ladder from researcher to reporter to editor. That was in 1995, at the dawn of the internet and a perfect moment to be working as a tech journalist. She was just twenty-six when she was hired as the editor in chief of a new publication called *WebWeek*. Five months later, she let herself be wooed away by another startup magazine called *Yahoo! Internet Life*. Over the next few years, Gunn wrote for a number of well-regarded trade publications—columns for *IEEE Internet Computing* and *Computer Shopper*, product reviews for *PC Magazine*— before moving to Seattle, in 1999, for a job as tech editor at the city's big alternative weekly, the *Seattle Weekly*. That was at the peak of Microsoft's industry might and a couple of years after a relatively modest-sized online books-and-CD retailer named Amazon had gone public. At the *Weekly*, Gunn wrote a column she called Kiss My ASCII (ASCII— pronounced "ass-C" or "ass-key," depending on whom you ask—is a computer standard for text dating back to the 1960s) and also contributed to its film and music sections.

Gunn never seemed to stay in one place long. Two years after moving to Seattle she was back in New York to rejoin the staff of *Yahoo! Internet Life*, which went out of business a year later. There was a brief stint as tech editor of *TimeOut New York* before Gunn moved to the Washington, D.C. area to take over as tech editor of *USA Today*, a national newspaper with a circulation in the millions. That proved a great job but also a burnout position and one that allowed her little time for her own writing. She stepped down as tech editor but continued writing for the paper and its website. She also moved back to Seattle, where she cohosted a short-lived revival of *PC World's Digital Duo*, a PBS tech show focused on new products. At its peak, it ran on 184 public television stations around the country. "There's always part of me that craves the new thing," Gunn said.

Digital Duo was canceled at the end of 2005. Gunn thought about moving back to New York but she landed a gig with *Computerworld*, which wanted her to stay on the West Coast. Her interests were growing geekier, as were the outlets interested in publishing her work. Her change in focus meant a return to the more esoteric publications where she launched her journalism career. "As a journalist, I was looking into privacy," Gunn said. "That led to security issues, and I was off to the races."

The job at Microsoft was a happy accident. "I wasn't looking for them and they weren't looking for me specifically, either," she said. A friend—someone who had written for her at *Computerworld*—had met with someone at Microsoft to talk about a new position working with some of its security people. The friend said he didn't think he was right for the job but recommended Gunn. "Microsoft reached out to me to gauge my interest and I figured what the hell." She knew Microsoft well from two decades of reporting and they knew her work. "They told me they felt I'd been pretty evenhanded in my coverage over the years," she said, but they also couldn't refrain from quoting a couple of sharp things she had written. In 2010, twenty years after she had taken her first job in journalism, Gunn showed up on Microsoft's campus to work as a senior response communications manager within the company's Trustworthy Computing program, which Bill Gates himself had announced, in the early 2000s, once the company belatedly decided to get serious about security. Gunn was now working incident response for the world's largest software maker, a very fat target for people with bad intentions.

"WE'RE SOMEWHERE BETWEEN A firefighter and dental hygienist," Gunn said of those who work incident response. The firefighter part of the job means rushing in when clients fear the worst about their computer systems—a member of the "cyber special forces," as Gunn's latest company, the London-based BAE Systems, describes the four thousand people working for them across the globe to "defend against cyber-attacks, fraud, and financial crime."* It's that part of the job that prompts Gunn and others to make comparisons to paramedics, ER doctors, and other first responders. The dental hygienist part of the job is the preventative work Gunn does. She's responsible for a small constellation of clients. Are they making security a priority

---

* "Our Vision," BAE Systems, https://www.baesystems.com/en/cyber security/about-us/our-vision#.

and investing the resources and time needed to reinforce and test their defenses (and thereby reduce the likelihood that she'll need to play heroine because its defenses have been compromised)? "It's a strange balance," she notes. "The IR [incident response] work is pure firefighting. But the 'readiness' part of the job"—how incident response people spend much of their time—"is really about the importance of flossing and periodic checkup appointments," she said. This time between incidents is a time for healing. "We call that polish-the-firetruck time," Gunn said.

Most people spend only a few years, if that, in incident response. Just as emergency rooms are common entry points for recent medical school grads doing the internship or residency they must endure to become a doctor, so is incident response a standard route for people getting into info-sec. "When people ask me, 'How do I get into this field?' I tell them, 'Go get an on-call gig,'" said Cisco's Craig Williams. "Not at a help desk but something where you're working on these breaking security issues." For people at Cisco or Microsoft or Google, that means responding to news of a vulnerability in one of their products. A software team will work on a fix but meanwhile a quick patch must be applied, a makeshift intrusion prevention system deployed, and an autopsy performed to figure out what happened. At a firm like Gunn's, it's her and her team responding to an "incident," which is what people in the industry tend to call it when a client phones to report a problem. The hours can be brutal but the pay excellent, even for those with little or no experience in info-sec. The average pay for an entry-level "incident analyst/responder" in 2018, according to CyberSeek's Cybersecurity Career Pathway, was $99,000 a year, and yet there are thousands of openings in the field. Entry-level forensic work—what the survey describes as a "cybercrime analyst/investigator"—was paying $85,000 a year. Salaries are bound to be inflated for those fortunate enough, financially at least, to work in a big city for a huge corporation or a big international consulting firm.

"Frankly, it's a job a lot of people burn out on," said Cisco's Williams. "But it's one of those positions where you learn a ton. If you're just getting into the field, it's a great way to get up to speed." Williams knew it wasn't the right life for him early in his career at Cisco, when he and his wife were relatively new to Austin and out at a place called Trudy's, known for selling margaritas so oversized that they cut you off at two. "I make it my personal challenge to finish two every time," Williams told me. He had already polished off his second margarita when his cell phone went off. It was his boss. "He's like, 'There's a worm in Thailand; we need you to come in and write an update,'" Williams said. He explained that he was in no condition to drive, let alone write a patch, but his boss wasn't accepting his no. "So my wife drives me to the office and I write the update as she sits there looking at me like, 'You have the weirdest job.'" Williams is still with Cisco as a company "director," where he plays more of an ambassador role and not what anyone would describe as an on-call job. "That was my life when I first joined the company," he said. "But as you can imagine, that's not a super-sustainable model."

Yet there are also people like Gunn, for whom incident response, if not the perfect job, seems as good as it gets in a world where you have to devote fifty or sixty or more hours every week to pay the bills and keep the lights on. "It's a work style that feels comfortable to me," Gunn said, adding, "I'd rather be summoned on a call at four in the morning a few times a year than sit there in a nine-to-five job being bored." She had worked as a deadline journalist and agreed with me when I offered that her job now seems not unlike all those years she was working for websites in the business of breaking news. When I asked her if she's happy doing what she's doing, she laughed. "Have you ever known a truly happy journalist, ER worker, or first responder?" she countered. I conceded the point but then Gunn gave a direct answer to my question: "It's a lot of crazy hours. Sometimes I'm surviving on caffeine. But I do like it. I'm enjoying it."

Gunn had always been a talented journalist. So it was no surprise that she had the right instincts about security back when she was still writing about tech: she was writing increasingly about security in the second half of the 2000s, just as the computing world was moving in that direction. Security—along with privacy issues—was becoming more central to computing and becoming a greater priority inside the industry. News outlets started employing reporters who focused exclusively on security. Venture capitalists funded more security startups while more traditional corporate security companies that had always focused on physical security beefed up their cyber practice. So, too, did big-name accountant firms and other consultancies. And Microsoft was hardly alone. Every big name in computing, from Apple to Google to Facebook, has suffered embarrassing data breaches.

Microsoft was eight years into its transformation from security laggard to industry leader when Gunn joined the company. Gates had implemented Microsoft's Trustworthy Computing program in 2002, and twelve months later, the "Slammer" worm hit one of Microsoft's core products, SQL Server, the database software that helps run business around the world—"the storage backend," as a former Microsoft engineer described it for me. Slammer infected roughly seventy-five thousand servers in ten minutes and caused problems across the globe, including flight delays and clogged ATM networks. "That caused Bill G [Bill Gates] to declare a major reset," the engineer said. "The whole company stopped working on features, at least for a bit, and focused on security." The job Gunn had been recruited to fill was created both to improve communications about security issues with the company's developer community and also those who were using Microsoft products.

Gunn was on the job six weeks when the world learned about Stuxnet, one of the more insidious worms to ever infect computers connected to the internet. Inspectors for the International Atomic Energy Agency found that centrifuges at an Iranian uranium enrichment plant were failing at alarming rates yet couldn't figure out why. Several months later, computers around the world were spontaneously crashing and rebooting. That was Stuxnet, which took advantage of multiple security holes in Windows and other software. The brilliance of Stuxnet was twofold. First, it covered its tracks. It hid the malicious files it added to a computer and took extra steps to cloak any processes it was initiating. Second, Stuxnet weaponized a computer: it didn't steal information or wipe out a hard drive but instead hid out and did physical destruction to the Iranian nuclear facility—the world's first digital weapon, reportedly created by Israel and the United States to disrupt Iran's nuclear efforts.

"Stuxnet was my first big case," Gunn said. "That was brutal." The fact that she was so new to the field only added to the "weirdness," she said. "My poor boss. We weren't close but he says to me, 'You do this, you're not going to be a journalist anymore.' This is a month or two into Stuxnet. He asks me, 'You sure you want to do this? Because if you want to go back, we can pretend this never happened.' Basically, he was asking me, 'Are you in or are you out?'"

Gunn wasn't going anywhere. There was something intoxicating about being on the inside after all those years as a journalist on the outside. She had found out about Stuxnet before most of the rest of the world when she was summoned to what she called the "ssirp room." (A shortened version of what at Microsoft they call the Software Security Incident Response Process, or SSIRP.) Weeks passed before they pieced together what had happened. "We're talking meetings that lasted for hours with people you're scared to make eye contact with because they're screaming," she said. "But you start to figure out what's going. What's on fire and needs immediate attention and what can wait until tomorrow." There were showers downstairs for those days when there was no time to make it home. "All of us had a locker for a change of clothes. There were nap rooms. A towel service. Food. It wasn't uncommon to spend three days on-site."

Gunn coordinated communication for the company's incident response group. Much of the job boiled down to managing how Microsoft spoke to the wider world about Stuxnet or some other piece of malware introduced through a security flaw in a company product. Often that plan centered on a speech delivered in a large ballroom at one of the big industry conferences: Black Hat, Hack in the Box, RSA. Gunn fielded press calls on security-related topics, and handled communications from contractors, consultants, third-party software makers, and others outside the company. She provided answers when she could and, when she couldn't, routed the query to the right person. Gunn delivered regular security bulletins—one or two in a quiet month, a dozen or more in a busier one, and, when necessary, published a special advisory. She blogged about security issues on the Microsoft website and served as a writing coach and editor for members of her group who wanted to write about whatever small disaster hit Windows or another Microsoft product.

Yet the part of the job Gunn loved—the part she spoke of with passion years later—were the hours spent in the ssirp room after they had learned of a new security breach. "There's this excitement," she said. "You're constantly on the phone, figuring out what's happening, getting your guys together, getting control of this thing." She was fascinated by the glimpses it gave into the people she worked with: those who rose to the occasion and those who couldn't handle the pressure. "A lot of incident response training comes from watching people who are really good at it do it," she said. A small incident might mean only a few days in the room but the drama stretched out for weeks when it was a massive problem like Stuxnet. "You worked on an issue you were assigned to until it was time to stand down," Gunn said. Some chafed at that kind of pressure but Gunn seemed to thrive on it. "When I shifted to another position inside Microsoft, I missed it," she said. Sitting across from me at Bedlam Coffee, she mimed out the feeling she had once she had shifted to that new job at Microsoft. She stared longingly at a make-believe door now off-limits and then said in falsetto, as if a child, "You mean I can't go into the ssirp room anymore?"

Gunn's first job in info-sec ended when, a little over two and a half years after she had started at Microsoft, in the fall of 2012 she received a promotion from senior response communications manager to senior security strategist. Her job now was to help Microsoft figure out how it should talk to the larger world about vulnerabilities in its software. She represented the company at conferences, promoted interesting research being conducted at Microsoft, and helped introduce "bug bounty" programs to college campuses. This last initiative proved a radical shift for any software maker. Rather than fight the impulse of hackers to find holes in a product, Microsoft would pay a reward to any who reported a vulnerability in its software.

Yet the commute from her home in Seattle across Lake Washington to Redmond, where Microsoft is headquartered, was taking a toll, as was workplace drama inside the company's security unit. Fifteen months after her promotion, Gunn left Microsoft for Hewlett-Packard, where her friend Dave Weinstein, whom she had met while both were working security at Microsoft, had landed a year earlier. HP had taken custody of the Zero Day Initiative, an effort by white-hat hackers to create a kind of clearinghouse of software flaws that lead to cyberattacks and security breaches. There, Weinstein was among those analyzing the bugs that researchers sent to Zero Day in the hopes of being paid a bounty for finding a security flaw. "We told you how much we were willing to pay for the bug and the researcher said yes or no," Weinstein said. "If they said yes, that meant they sold us the intellectual property in the bug, and then we would study it and use it" to better combat malware. The attraction for Gunn was a chance to work "threat intelligence" and, not incidentally, take a break from the intensity of IR work inside a place like Microsoft. She didn't go to HP thinking she was done with IR but she was happy for the time away. "People cycle in and out all the time," Gunn said. Once again, she was working as a writer and editor. She oversaw the white papers, blog posts, public speeches, and tweets produced by Zero Day engineers while also publishing her own original research.

Gunn enjoyed working at HP. The hours were good, her colleagues congenial, the work interesting. There were also holidays with family. "Most people in IR can't remember a December holiday that went without a hitch," she said. "There are always calls on Christmas and Thanksgiving, even when I was covering this stuff as a journalist." Yet she also missed being in the room and the camaraderie that came with doing battle against a formidable new bug. There were also the good feelings that came with a job that let Gunn compare herself to the gunslinger in an old-time western who saves the town from the bad guys. "There's something wonderful about rolling in and playing the hero," she said.

In November 2016, nearly three years after she started at HP, Gunn went to work for BAE Systems Applied Intelligence. Microsoft had seemed old compared to Google and Facebook when she had gone to work there in 2010. Hewlett-Packard, which dates back to the late 1930s, seemed ancient by comparison. Yet BAE's roots, she learned during her orientation, dated back to the 1500s. "I figure my next move will be the Vatican," Gunn said.

WHILE I WAS IN Seattle, I asked Gunn to walk me through a recent case. She graciously complied, so long as I promised not to name the company or provide any revealing details such as location or relative size. We agreed I would refer to the client generically as a "financial institution." They had contacted Gunn a month or so earlier, when they discovered that sensitive files might had been filched—no small issue for a financial institution that handles sensitive client information and operates under the watchful eye of regulators. "I see people in some of the worst twenty-four, forty-eight, or seventy-two hours of their life," Gunn said. "They've got bosses yelling at them, they're dealing with lawyers, they're worried about the regulators. They've let everyone down, and they're feeling bad about themselves."

The case involved a "rogue employee," which instantly put a frown on her face. "My least favorite kind of case," she said. They're messier than other cases, and typically more fraught with emotion. "The human element can make it really painful. People are dealing with betrayal on top of everything else." Someone inside—a colleague, and therefore someone they know—has done something wrong. And now Gunn and her team would be upending everyone's life to ascertain how much damage had been done and unearth what they might know about what happened. "In this case, the supervisor is looking at this as a personal betrayal," she said.

The employee in question had already been on the financial institution's watch list—on administrative review for poor performance. Going back over old e-mails, which as Gunn points out is their right under the employment contract the woman had signed, they saw that she had sent unknown documents to her home computer, contrary to explicit corporate policy and possibly in violation of state and federal regulations. "They weren't sure what she took or why," Gunn said. "They just knew that there was a non-zero instance of that." Non-zero? "It had happened at least once," she said.

Gunn had been working with this client since shortly after she started at BAE and knew them well from the training sessions she had performed with its people. Called "tabletops," that's where Gunn walked the client through a series of war-games-like exercises. They tested their defenses, challenged the procedures and decision-making processes they had in place, and went over the protocols for documenting any anomalies should they occur. "Their regulators and accreditors require that they have planning in place," she said, but it's also mandatory in the digital age. "Assume a breach," she said. "Assume something bad happens. You can't live your charmed life forever. Nobody does.

"Organizations, if they have it together, prepare for these kinds of things," she continued. "This one had a plan. They had procedures in place." The question was whether they had been following those procedures—or, more realistically, how far short had they fallen measured by the written standards enshrined in the playbooks and procedure manuals the financial institution had created for its people. "On that first call, basically my job is to listen. I'm sitting on the phone with my main contact there, basically interviewing her, trying to figure out what they know. I'm also trying to assess the threat level. Do they have a bad feeling about this, is this person bad news?"

The lowest threat level would be an "event," which is info-sec speak for "something has happened to a computer." Maybe a machine keeps crashing or network issues are preventing people from accessing a website. Those are both events. An "incident" implies a security angle. A computer that repeatedly crashes because of memory management problems is an event. One that crashes because a virus has infected the system would be deemed an incident. A security "breach" is the worst kind of incident: when confidential data has been copied (stolen) or otherwise compromised by someone without authorization to view that material. Invariably a bad breach is privacy-related and involves credit cards, passwords, and other confidential documents. "This was certainly an incident," Gunn said. "The question was whether there had been a breach." Had loan data been compromised? Customer data? "If that's the case, then we're talking about a four-alarm fire. That's bad breachy. That's criminal activity; that means getting law enforcement involved, along with lawyers and regulators."

This first call lasted well over an hour. Gunn walked her contact through the immediate steps the financial institution needed to take to contain the damage. The primary focus was on the rogue employee who, after all, was an insider with privileged access to the system. Gunn imagined the worst. Maybe the woman was a disgruntled employee thinking about infecting the computer system with malware. Maybe she sought client data in order to gain access to their accounts. "We have no idea at this point what she did, or why, but we've got to take basic first steps: cut off her access, lock out her passwords, make sure her employee pass is disabled so she can't get in the building," Gunn said. Even if a pass is disabled, a determined adversary can still get inside—through a bit of social engineering (for instance, talking their way into the building by claiming they had misplaced the now-disabled employee pass) or drafting closely behind someone with an active pass. She counseled her contact to make that extra call to front-desk security to let them know what was going on.

The targeted employee was in regular contact with the institution's internet service provider. Gunn learned this during that first conversation. "Call them and say they shouldn't take her calls right now," Gunn said. There was no need to tell them much more than that, other than they were still trying to figure out what happened. She also suggested they reach out to the woman's clients with the same message. Mainly the two were all business but Gunn's style was such that her boss teases her about being a kind of IT therapist. "I'm always sure to ask, 'How are you feeling? Are you okay?'" she said.

Gunn phoned the client a couple of hours later. By this time it was late in the afternoon in what promised to be a very long day. Gunn wanted to check on her progress but also comfort someone whom she recognized was having a very bad day. "'Okay, you've done this, you've done that, you've done all these things, you're doing great,'" Gunn told the woman. This has always been her style, the small-town Nebraska girl now in the role of high-priced security specialist, all encouragement and positive reinforcement. They went over other steps the woman could take that evening and Gunn reassured her that she was hard at work on her end. "I tell her, 'I'm working on things on my end, I'm getting my team together, we're working on getting someone out to her fast.'" A few hours later her contact at the financial institution was calling her: "Can you talk to my CIO for a few minutes?" The company's chief information officer wanted to check in that night, Gunn said, "because panic goes up the food chain." If anything, Gunn was relieved it was only around nine o'clock. It's routine in cases like this, she said, to get calls at eleven or midnight. A year earlier, she worked with a European-based client whose U.S.-based operations had suffered a bad breach. "I was sleeping in two-hour blocks, which is not a recipe for sane behavior. After a week of that, I was like, 'You know what, your entire nation can collapse for all I care, I need some uninterrupted sleep.'"

Gunn was one or two weeks into another case when she picked up this one. She was also doing mop up on a third. "You get very good at juggling," she said. Despite these other cases, there were several lengthy phone calls the next day, both with people on her side and with the client. Her contact at the financial institution told her that because there was a branch office near where the offending employee lived, they had also contacted security there to give them the heads-up on what was happening. That provided another opportunity for Gunn to offer positive reinforcement. "I complimented her on doing me one better," she said. "I told her, 'That's great, that's fantastic.'" Yet that same day she learned that the company wasn't keeping a log of every e-mail, which, among other things, would capture the name of every document sent out as an attachment and the name of the person or people who sent it. Gunn acted out the moment by making an audible gulping sound, sighing loudly, and then flashing a fake smile. "My job at that point is to say, 'Okay, we'll address that later when we make some recommendations.'" Besides serving as taskmaster and IT therapist, her job requires that she also be a part-time diplomat.

Others in incident response are not near as gentle in their approach. Gunn tells of someone she worked with early in her time at BAE. "I don't think he liked my style, and I sure as shit didn't like his. Growly, yelling at people, making them feel stupid," she said, the clients included.

"Unlike some other people in threat intel, I don't like to raise the drama," Gunn said. "I like to lower the drama. Because drama gets in the way of you solving stuff." There's also what she called "the human side" to the interactions she has. "I sympathize with what they're going through. They're under tremendous stress, it's traumatic, and, in this case, you've got the added drama that the person in question is someone they've probably had coffee with. She probably knows her kids' names."

Gunn spent some of this second day reading through months of e-mails written by the rogue insider. "I now know what crazy looks like," she cracked when telling me the story. The next time she spoke to her contact, she was sure to ask, "How's the mood in the office today?" There was a deliberateness to the query. She was probing for the possibility that the woman had allies in the office who might inadvertently agree to act as her co-conspirator and unwittingly help her purloin more documents. "How did people react when you told them the news?" she asked. The answer in this case helped Gunn lower the threat level. People seemed generally relieved to be rid of a problematic coworker, the woman told her. Gunn also asked if the employee in question was good with computers and felt relieved to hear she wasn't. She wouldn't have to worry about digital time bombs that may have been left behind just in case her access to the system was cut off.

One limit of Gunn's job is one that confronts all outside consultants. She's a trusted advisor but only an advisor. "You're leading the investigation but you're not," she said. She can encourage people to follow her advice but not order them to do so. Add to that the limits that come from sitting in Seattle and not being on-site to check whether a client has followed through on any of her recommendations. A year or so earlier, she had warned a client about a company they were acquiring because they used a tool that raised security concerns. "They say, 'Oh, don't worry, we're decommissioning that, let's not waste time on that,'" Gunn said. "Four months later, they had their asses handed to them by that thing that wasn't worth wasting time on."

Gunn sometimes had to fight the urge to snap at the client. It wasn't just the client's failure to maintain e-mail logs. During that first conversation, she had asked if the rogue insider had any company equipment in her possession. Told no, Gunn had crossed that item off her list of things to worry about. But her contact amended that statement two days later. A review showed that the woman had logged out a company laptop for a job but there was no record of her returning it—another item to add to the post-op client memo Gunn was already writing in her head. Another time it was the client's failure to speak to a lawyer. With me she said out loud what she couldn't quite tell the client: "Remember two days ago when I said you need to talk to counsel before you do this? And the part where you didn't do that? Okay, so now this is the new reality we're working in."

Despite these and other glitches, Gunn was lowering the threat level she maintained in her head. The only documents that seemed to have made their way outside the company's perimeters included sensitive information but Gunn concluded there had been no breach—nothing like passwords or social security numbers had been copied. "Instantly, the CIO is breathing a sigh of relief," she said. "Because that means not having to write one of those bad letters to your customers saying you messed up." Everything she was hearing about the targeted employee was about how she was a know-it-all who thought she was smarter than those above her on the org chart. The targeted woman's boss—not the woman she was in conversation with throughout but another woman, if that mattered—was insisting that she review documents before sending them to clients. Maybe sending herself the documents was an act of independence, or of defiance or hubris—*I'll do what I damn well please with the documents I'm working on.* Maybe she didn't know that sending a client's sensitive information over an open network was against the rules or just didn't care.

"At some point, I have to let go of motive," Gunn said. "Why did this woman do this? Who knows? She might be a bitey spider that can poison me. I don't know, but I have a jar over it and it can't hurt anyone so fuck it."

The client had its own IT people. They were already combing through the system, piecing together what happened, and looking for any irregularities. But Gunn had offered to dispatch one of her techs and the client said yes: "They wanted my guy in. 'Have him sit with us and look at logs. We need fresh eyes.'" Gunn thought it was a good idea to send in a neutral party "rather than all these people who knew this woman and now were being asked to be involved in an investigation against her." A junior-level analyst would have sufficed but she wanted to send her tech lead who, if not exactly charismatic, had a soothing presence. "I gravitate toward that type. People I know I can send out who won't make the situation worse," Gunn said. "He's very comforting in his way."

Yet Gunn's number two had been waylaid by another client whose system, in Gunn's term, "was full of botulism. And Ebola." Before visiting the financial institution, he first needed to scrub clean this other client's systems and, Ghostbusters-style, capture the various viruses and vermin on a hard drive. "To study it and better understand the kind of stuff we had to defend against," said Gunn. That meant waiting an extra day, which is its own kind of stress. "I had talked it all through with the client," Gunn said. "The spider was under the glass. They were fine with the delay." Three days after the financial institution's initial call, one of her people was finally on-site. "By that point, he's just sitting with the client to hold their hand through everything," she said. "He's there for a day, reassuring them he's checking out everything and that everything's okay."

Gunn still had additional work before she could close the case. There were more phone calls and the report she needed to write, along with recommendations for improving security. Nothing serious had happened yet Gunn disagreed when I referred to the case as a "minor one." "When your CIO is standing in your office asking questions and you're on the phones with lawyers, nothing about the experience feels minor," she said. She didn't need to break terrible news to her client but what she would be writing in her report would hardly make them happy. She quoted an old colleague of hers from her days at Microsoft. "We're here to make a terrible day only a bad one or a bad day not so bad," Gunn said. "The joke is you never get good days in our line of work. But at least you can say that at least there's no trash cans on fire anymore and for that a client will be grateful."

2

THE SNIFFER

The client was a financial giant—a top-five bank known to practically everyone on earth. Mark Seiden's task was to see if he could steal some of its most precious documents. This global behemoth booked tens of billions of dollars in revenues each year and had in its employ a small squadron of former police, military, and security officers. Yet it was no match for this short, bespectacled man with a gift for computers and the moxie of a grifter.

"Tell me the things you most want to keep secret," Seiden challenged the executive who had hired him. He listed two. One was the identities of clients negotiating deals so hush-hush that even people inside the bank referred to them using code names. The other was the fees they charged for their work. The executive handed Seiden the same ID the bank would issue any contractor or employee, giving him twenty-four-hour access to the building. The question the bank had was whether it made itself vulnerable to a serious breach each time it brought on a consultant or new employee. "Most systems are like a Tootsie Pop," Seiden said. "They have this hard, crunchy outside but they're very gooey and soft on the inside. Once you get past that crunchy outside and you're inside, you can do anything."

The first thing Seiden did was log on to a computer and probe the bank's digital defenses. Invariably, that was step one. He used scanning tools to reveal any obvious vulnerabilities: whether the organization was using a default password or a weak one, or whether its IT people had failed to install a known patch. When those didn't reveal any security holes, he resorted to plan B, or what he called "the physical thing." He would try to obtain the bank's secrets in the physical world rather than over a computer network.

Seiden began showing his face at the bank during the day to get people used to seeing him while also scoping things out. Mainly, though, he worked at night, when there weren't prying eyes watching what he was doing. Perusing an employee directory, he figured out where the head of facilities worked. "This guy has a title like associate vice president but no private office," Seiden said. He located the man's work area, where he found a locked cabinet. Using a paperclip, Seiden broke into it. Inside, he found floor plans and keys to its facilities around the world. He copied the floor plans before putting them back. The keys he took.

Another find during one of these nocturnal scavenger hunts was the bank's backup tapes, boxed and ready for pickup. This was pre–"cloud computing," when businesses backed up their computer files on thick magnetic tape generally stored at another location. "So I walked away with a set of backups," he said. Later, he was shocked that the information on the tapes had not been encrypted. "You'd think a company like that would know to encrypt its backup tapes," he said, shaking his head. With a cheap tape reader picked up at any Office Depot or Staples, he could mine the confidential customer data on the purloined tapes.

On another night, Seiden visited the cubicle of the employee in charge of the bank's phone system. "There are lots of secrets on voice mails," he said. "So I thought it'd be really cool to get voice-mail passwords." Theoretically, with those in hand, he could listen to messages left for the CEO and those occupying other top positions—the bank's top lawyer, say, or the executive running mergers and acquisitions. That might get him closer to the information he was after but, he said, "there are certain lines I won't cross." He'd let the client know what he had found but not use the passwords to eavesdrop on private conversations.

Seiden used the stolen keys to gain access to the accounting department. There he found a list of code names, handed out to mask the names of its biggest deals. The clerk who handled them kept them in an unlocked file draw next to her desk, and why not? She worked in a locked office, so why keep the file in a locked cabinet? With the list of code names in hand and a bit more digging, he found out how much the bank was charging the client on each project.

Yet what were the clients' real names? That required a bit of social engineering. "People will tell you almost anything if they see you're calling from an inside extension," he said. Pretending to be a banker, he said he was initiating a project that needed a code name: Who should he contact? That weekend he visited the man's desk. "Sure enough, there was a filing cabinet that had everything I needed," he said. "I copied it all." That's when he told his contact at the bank that he was ready for another meeting.

ever breaches. Post-Yahoo, he was once again a free agent cobbling together a living. He took a part-time job as director of security for 1010data, a data management and analytics firm, and has carved out a nice side business as a forensic witness in court cases that involve computers. That's been a "late in life thing," he said, "because that's when you're really an expert." The work pays well and also lets him feel like he's playing detective, except he gets to do his sleuthing by exploring the contents of hard drives while wearing pajamas. He also advertises on a site called angle .co, where he describes himself as a "security guru" happy to work as a trusted advisor to your startup.

"I'll take on any new cool problem that interests me," Seiden said. He's also a lecturer at the UC Berkeley School of Information and an "affiliate" at Stanford's Center for International Security and Cooperation, "which mostly means I get to hang out with classy people and occasionally do something useful with a student."

Nowadays, Seiden only rarely takes on a pen-testing assignment. One reason for this is a changing landscape. The idea of hiring outsiders to test a business's digital defenses was a relatively new field when Seiden first got into it in the latter half of the 1990s. Back then pen testers were free agents. Since then, the large accounting firms and private security companies have gotten into the business. Now there are businesses like FireEye that employ hundreds of pen testers they job out to their corporate clients. Another reason: Seiden's heart just isn't in it as in the past. Maybe he's aged out of a job that occasionally has him dressing up as a FedEx delivery man. In his more cynical moments, he wonders if his assaults on a company's defenses measure the cleverness of people like him more than anything else. "I recommend to a company that if it has $30,000 to spend, use it for a design review rather than a pen test," he said.

That's not to say he's against the idea of a business periodically hiring outsiders to probe for vulnerabilities. "If a corporation has never done penetration testing, that to me is a big red flag. Why not? Do they have something to hide? Are they in denial? Are they scared what you might find out?"

3

THE SECURITY PRINCESS

"Information security engineer" sounded so boring. Parisa Tabriz figured she could do better than that title when, in 2011, she was promoted to a management position. Officially, she was an information security engineer overseeing the information security engineering team. "I thought it was a mouthful and also so dry," Tabriz said. Around a year into the new position, she attended a big security conference in Tokyo and needed business cards for a country where exchanging them is a central ritual. Using Google's internal website to order business cards, she discovered how easy it was to change her title: fill in whatever you wanted. Others she knew dubbed themselves "hacker for hire" or some other more whimsical self-bestowed honorific. On the spot, she decided to declare herself "Security Princess." To this day, that's her de facto title, both inside Google and to the wider world.

"It's a great icebreaker," said Tabriz, thirty-five, but also an ironic moniker. "I'm not stereotypically princessy," she confessed. She grew up with two brothers and was "a bit of a tomboy." She played a lot of video games, she said, and a lot of sports. She was "one of the guys in college," which is where she stumbled onto computer security as a potential career choice. Her personal website was so badly infected that it was serving up Viagra ads, "and I had to find out why."

TABRIZ WASN'T THE COMPUTER nerd whose life was forever changed the first time she touched a PC. There was a family computer in her house growing up in the Chicago suburbs in the 1990s, but she felt nothing like magic when it was her turn to use it. "I remember playing computer games and using *Encarta* [the first popular digital encyclopedia] to do research," she said, and using AOL Instant Messenger (AIM) to talk with friends. She did well in math and science but "I also liked art classes a lot." Her father was a doctor who had grown up in Iran and immigrated to the United States as a young man. Her mother is Polish American and works as a nurse. When applying to college, Tabriz had no idea what she wanted to do except she knew she didn't want to go into medicine like her parents. "My parents are fairly conservative, culturally, politically, and in every other way," she noted. "So I think maybe there's an element of rebellion in me as the oldest." She can't be sure, she added, "but I can imagine that rebelliousness being related in some way to my ending up in security."

Strong math and science scores secured her an acceptance to the University of Illinois at Urbana-Champaign, home to one of the top-ranked computer science programs in the country. She would declare herself a computer engineering major almost by default. "I think it's kind of crazy that you have to decide what you wanna be when you're what, sixteen or seventeen, but I was like, 'Well, this is something relevant that I can spend a lot of time on, and it could be interesting to learn about. And because I don't know what else to do.'" Despite her declared major, she arrived on campus, she said, not knowing the difference between a browser and AOL. Much of the tech world had already migrated to Google by the time she started college but not Tabriz, who was still using its predecessor, an old search engine called AltaVista. "AOL was the internet to me," she said.

College meant no longer sharing a computer with her brothers and parents. "Unlimited [internet] access opened up music, via BitTorrent, which got me learning how BitTorrent worked because that was kind of cool technology," Tabriz said. She was attending one of the country's most elite engineering schools, famous for graduates such as Marc Andreessen, who coauthored Mosaic, the first widely used internet browser, and then cofounded Netscape, and Max Levchin, who stands as one of Silicon Valley's more incredible serial entrepreneurs (a cofounder of PayPal in the late 1990s and now his seventh startup, which has a paper value of $1.5 billion). Yet a lot of what she was learning, Tabriz said, came through the free tutorials she found via whatever browser she might have been using at the time. "At some point I wanted to do journalism or art," she said. "But my parents were like, 'No, you will be a starving artist, you need to become a doctor or an engineer.'" She created a personal web page by teaching herself HTML and JavaScript. "I thought maybe I could do graphic design," she said. "It was tech, so it was respectable, and also art."

The hacking of her website changed everything. She already belonged to the campus web development club but joined a second one devoted to security issues. "I basically started asking questions," Tabriz said. "Why would someone do this? Oh, because they can make money this way. And how did this happen? Oh, because I didn't take this extra step." She was hooked, she said. She changed majors from computer engineering—a hardware concentration—to computer science, which meant a software focus. She also spent a lot more time working with others in her security club, learning more about web and system security. While still in school, she attended DEF CON, the annual hacker conference in Las Vegas. "That exposed me to hacking and other types of computer security," said Tabriz, who spent an extra year on campus to earn a master's in computer science.

"So much of information security is about checking assumptions," Tabriz noted. A programmer writes a small bit of code, thinking people will use the system in the way they intend it to be used but others find ways in or clever workarounds. "The hacker can break those assumptions and get the system to work in a way that was never intended."

There's an element of serendipity in every person's tale. A job as a lifeguard at a community pool while she was still in school had her sometimes scraping dried nacho cheese off the counter at the concession stand. That led to a job as system administrator for a dorm on campus, which helped her land a summer internship with a large pharmaceutical company. "That was one of the most valuable career-related experiences of my life," Tabriz declared. She disliked the experience so much that "it veered me strongly in another direction." She came across a cybersecurity internship posting on a digital bulletin board at school—an experience that proved critical when applying for a job at Google. "It probably gave me just enough relevant job experience for someone at Google to consider me for an interview," she said. Her decision to even apply for a job there was no more profound than her preference for Gmail and Google as a search engine. "I just thought, 'Wouldn't it be cool to work at a company whose products I was using?'" Shortly before her graduation from the University of Illinois in 2006, she applied for an intern position on the company's security team.

There's great mystery shrouding the Google interview process. There are the brain stumpers meant to show people how you think. "You have a 3 gallon jug and 5 gallon jug," a Googler might ask. "How do you measure out exactly 4 gallons?"* Candidates stand for a lot of their interviews, at a whiteboard with marker in hand, walking someone through an engineering puzzle, posed to hear the candidate engage in a technical discussion. Often a candidate meets with four or more people—and by the end of the process is wrung dry.

But Tabriz was applying for an internship and one specifically in security. She had two interviews and both were conducted over the phone. "I remember wearing pajamas for both," she said—and a feeling of great relief at the end of them. They focused on the hows and whys of networking protocols and other nerdy security topics she knew well. "I don't remember any crazy logic puzzles. But I do know that my interview path was different from

---

* The CareerSidekick website provides the solution in an article called, "8 Tough Brain Teaser Interview Questions and Answers from Google, Apple and Facebook": We know we can't get the final result in the 3 gallon jug. It'll overflow. We need to end up with 4 gallons in the 5 gallon jug. First fill the 3 gallon jug. Then pour the 3 gallons into the 5 gallon jug. Now the 3 gallon jug is empty, and the 5 gallon jug has 3 gallons in it. Fill the 3 gallon jug again. Slowly pour into the 5 gallon jug. Only 2 gallons will fit because it already has 3. Now it's full. Exactly 1 gallon is left in the 3 gallon jug. Dump out the 5 gallon jug. Pour your 1 gallon into the 5 gallon jug. Fill up the 3 gallon jug one more time and pour it into the 5 gallon jug! You have exactly 4 gallons. https://careersidekick.com/brain-teaser-job-interview-questions-facebook-google-apple/.

the normal Google software engineering route since I was expressly being hired into security." At the end of her internship, there were two more interviews, which included what she called "coding puzzles," but she's convinced that it was her performance during her four months working inside Google that secured her the job. "I was so overjoyed when I got the offer, I didn't negotiate at all," she said. Landing a job at Google is the stuff of legend, but for her the trick seemed to be her decision to focus on security while still an undergraduate. She knew the topic well and had a master's from one of the country's top engineering schools. That was enough to get her inside, where she could prove herself.

HER FIRST JOB AT Google had her looking for vulnerabilities in its product line. For Tabriz it was something like love at first sight. "There's no rule book for finding problems with software," she said. "The job means you have to think like a hacker. And I'll tell you, it's kind of fun to find ways to break things."

Somehow, thinking like a criminal came naturally to Tabriz and others on her team. The challenge confronting her six-person team was getting others at Google to do the same. "We had this approach of finding vulnerabilities and then teaching other developers at Google how to avoid creating them in the first place." They ran "think like an attacker" classes that began with a challenge to their fellow programmers to figure out ways of hacking into a vending machine to get free snacks. Then they'd go over common software errors and how someone with bad intentions might exploit them. People, for instance, would create login forms but then fail to take basic steps to secure that process. They need to "sanitize" the login inputs—isolate the process so an adversary couldn't sneak in their malicious code through a user name or password box.

Tabriz's job title was information security engineer—Google-speak for any of the fifty or so engineers the company then had focused on security (today they have more than five hundred). But she might have more accurately been described as an evangelist. Her job along with others was spreading the gospel of computer security within the company. The idea was to fix not just the code but also the coders: if they could get Google's programmers thinking about security when writing a program, they could prevent vulnerabilities that are only discovered after the fact. A couple of years after she started, the company moved her to Switzerland, where she spent around eighteen months as an engineer and trainer, running mini security tutorials for offices around Europe and Asia. In 2010, Tabriz and a second Googler implemented what they called the Resident Hacker curriculum—a crash course in computer security. There were in-person training sessions and online tutorials for those who wanted to learn remotely. "We've created much more intensive classes where we teach people how to hack, where we say, 'Okay, hack this application.'" Their most advanced class has people attacking an application they've dubbed Gruyere that is intentionally riddled with tiny security holes. "That's a multiday class by the time people get through everything."

These days Tabriz works out of Google's main campus in Mountain View, near the center of Silicon Valley. Tabriz, now a top engineer at the company, met me in a conference room in a look-alike glass building on campus. Just five years after starting at the company, in 2011, she moved into management—or at least Google's version of management. Some days the tips of her black hair were dyed fuchsia, or streaked with red. She might put on a dress to give a speech (she wore an all-white, belted dress for her Black Hat keynote), but her daily uniform is jeans, casual shirts, and maybe a sweater if wanting to dress up for a meeting.

Her first job in management was running what people inside the company called Central Security. Her team helped with project design and did code review within Google, pointing out any potential vulnerabilities and suggesting fixes. She was overseeing thirty or so engineers, almost all of them men, but she was used to this as an older sister with two younger brothers. She had been bossing boys around from an early age, she told a reporter with *The Telegraph* in 2014. "They'd say I was a bully, but I played them at their own game, in sports on the field, and at video games," she said.* By that time, she had made *Forbes*'s 30 Under 30 list. Speaking invites were coming her way, as were requests from magazine writers seeking an interview.

"We try in vain to keep up with her, but mostly recognize quickly we'll fail," Maarten Van Horenbeeck, a fellow Google security manager from that time, said of Tabriz in a LinkedIn tribute. "Few make the *Forbes* '30 under 30'

---

* Josie Esnor, "Google's Top Secret Weapon—a Hacker They Call Their Security Princess," *The Telegraph*, October 4, 2014, https://www.telegraph.co.uk/technology/google/11140639/Googles-top-secret-weapon-a-hacker-they-call-their-Security-Princess.html.

list on a Friday, head out for a weekend climb in the ice mountains of the Sierra Nevada, hop over to Singapore on Tuesday to orchestrate a hacker competition, and still show up in the office back on Thursday morning with home-baked cookies and a smile, ready to fix the internet. That's Parisa," wrote Van Horenbeeck, who is now the chief information security officer at Zendesk, a customer service software company.

Tabriz worked Central Security for only eighteen months before taking the top security position inside Chrome, the company's web browser. That represented a shift for Tabriz. She was now responsible for a single product rather than serving as a consultant to anyone inside Google needing security services. She would also need to build her own team. There were only five people dedicated to security on the Chrome team when she took over—and all of them, to her chagrin, were traditional security people. "When I joined Chrome, the people I inherited were people who were good at finding bugs in code and not thinking as much about the user interface or the experience of users," she said. One of her first hires was a woman who had earned a PhD exploring ways of making security more intuitive and user-friendly by interviewing users and studying how they responded to warning messages. That team, focused on user research, is roughly fifty-fifty, men-to-women, she said—a rarity in today's tech world.

"If we don't understand human psychology, and if we don't make these security protections we've built comprehensible and simple to the widest range of people possible, we're going to fail in our attempts to make the internet safer," said Tabriz, who a couple of years into the job handed out "Department of Chromeland Security" hoodies to her staff. These days the Chrome security group numbers in the dozens and includes a more diverse and broader range of people, including those with backgrounds in design, physics, math, real estate, and psychology. "It's quite blurry in my world," she said.

And yet that's not enough, Tabriz remarked—good news for anyone interested in computer security as a career. If she has a complaint about the security industry, it's that it still doesn't draw from a wide enough pool of talent. "We're still limited in expertise in design and psychology and sociology," she said. "We don't have enough on that spectrum." She spoke, too, about the importance of a greater gender and racial balance in the war against the cyber bad guys. Different experiences and backgrounds are always a good thing, she said, when trying to better understand and counter those wearing black hats.

"There's this meme out there that you have to be some tech genius who's been coding since you were in diapers if you're going to make it in cybersecurity," Tabriz said. "I don't think that's the case. A lot make it through hard work and an interest in a niche area." There's a role in security for tech prodigy who have been coding since they were in elementary school, and she certainly has plenty of those working with her inside Chrome. "But one of the biggest challenges with security is that humans are often the weakest link," Tabriz noted. If security protections are inconvenient or get in people's way, they're not going to work. "Understanding how humans operate is critical to everything we do."

The stakes for Tabriz and her team are enormous. Google launched Chrome more than a decade after the so-called browser wars that pitted Netscape Navigator against Microsoft's Internet Explorer in the second half of the 1990s. But today it's the internet's top browser—by a long measure. Chrome, which is installed on more than two billion devices, had a 62 percent market share in 2018. Apple's Safari was the second most popular browser with a 15 percent market share, while Firefox, a descendant of Navigator developed by the Mozilla Foundation, was in third place with a 5 percent share.[*] Tabriz may crack wise about "fixing the internet" when they patch a vulnerability in a Google product but there's truth to the joke. Between the Google search bar and Chrome, the Android operating system, YouTube, and Waze, the popular GPS navigation system, Google is a lot of the way most of us consume the internet.

To fend off everyone from small-time thieves fishing for people's banking and credit card information to state-backed hackers, Tabriz has invoked a bug bounty program. Hackers outside the company can earn rewards of up to $15,000 for just reporting a vulnerability in Chrome, or as much as $100,000 for writing a working exploit. That has cost the company millions but it's also led to fixes for hundreds of bugs. "You want these people on your side, not working against you," she explained.

Yet Tabriz's main strategy for battling the bad guys has Google itself taking care of security on behalf of its users

---

[*] "Browser Market Share Worldwide July 2017," StatCounter GlobalStats, http://gs.statcounter.com/browswer-market-share#monthly-201707-201707-map.

by integrating protections into Chrome and applications shared across Google products, including authentication, autofill, and syncing, rather than relying on the human factor. For instance, malware-detecting technologies are now baked into Chrome, as are "silent" security updates, which Tabriz described as "automatic updates hopefully you don't know even happened."

And to the extent that there's no getting around the human factor, there's clearer messaging. Under Tabriz, Chrome has dropped the inscrutable padlock icon that aimed to help users gauge the safety of a website. It's been replaced with an alert-style advisory written in block letters and with splashes of red ("WARNING: THIS SITE MAY HARM YOUR COMPUTER!"). Tabriz likens her job to that of a car manufacturer thinking about auto safety. A user "needs to know the basics of how to operate a car, but we have also introduced safety features which hopefully kick in if you're about to skid out of control," she said. Eventually Google will take care of security not just for its customers but also computer engineers working with its products. "Ideally, developers won't even have to worry about security because we'll build software libraries that automatically do this validation for you."

Tabriz is no activist. But she also seems more than a little fed up with the maleness of her world. She felt the 2018 lineup of keynote speakers at RSA, another of the big security conferences, was too white and too male, so Tabriz and the security chief of Facebook hastily put together rival conference they called OURSA, which featured a decidedly more diverse panel of security experts. She's taught hacker basics to Girl Scouts and r00tz (DEF CON for kids) attendees, and these days plays a larger role in employee development within Google. She has mentored (and continues to mentor) young female Google engineers, and has also stepped up her efforts to recruit good people to computer security both from within the company and without. "A lot of the people we hire just have this curiosity to try to understand something," Tabriz told *Elle* in 2014, shortly after moving to Chrome. "And maybe a bit of a mischievous slant, to try to do something unexpected."*

Tabriz's role continued to expand at Google. In 2016 she was named director of engineering in charge of Chrome— or, as she cheekily proclaims on LinkedIn, the "Browser

---

* Clare Malone, "Meet Google's Security Princess," *Elle*, July 8, 2014, https://www.elle.com/culture/tech/a14652/google-parisa-tabriz-profile/.

Boss" inside the "House of Chrome." She now oversees the two hundred or so engineers assigned to Chrome—yet also reassures those who know her as the Security Princess, "I still do all that security and privacy stuff, too.

"If you're interested in having an impact on the world, I can think of few greater things than keeping people safe as they use technology," Tabriz said. "Technology is increasingly becoming part of everyone's lives, whether it's how you produce and share content with the world, how you buy things, how you do your banking, how you communicate with loved ones. It's so central to what we do and central to trying to keep people safe."

4

DEPARTMENT OF DEFENSE

Tea is among Dave Weinstein's most recent passions. So it's a tea shop on the eastern edge of Lake Washington that he has chosen for our meeting place, a mile from the outpost Google has established in Kirkland, Washington, just east of Seattle. There, the forty-eight-year-old Weinstein works as a manager in the company's Android security group. The LizzyKate tea shop is lovely and quaint, if not a bit precious for my tastes. It was also a terrible place for an interview. We sat at a wooden table in the middle of a shop stuffed with teapots, cups, and glass infusers that I feared might shatter as Weinstein, a large man with a booming voice, shared his story.

Angela Gunn, who had introduced us, described him as a "veteran of a Long Strange Trip." I think she meant the circuitous route that landed him in computer security, but meeting Weinstein in person made me think it was also a clever play on the phrase. Weinstein seemed the kind who a generation earlier might just have made anyone's list for most likely to join a long strange trip with the Grateful Dead. He's a large, burly man with long, dark hair and an unruly full beard, dressed in a tie-dye shirt and bulky cargo pants—pretty much his daily uniform. He lives in a small town in the foothills twenty miles from Google's offices, with his wife and two dachshunds, or three if you include the stray they have been caring for in the final months of her life. "There's a charity in western Washington called Old Dog Haven, which exists on the notion that dogs should not die in a shelter for the sin of being old," Weinstein explained. Nearly two years earlier, they had agreed to take in this newest addition to the family for the rest of her life. He is a man for whom an interest is all-consuming or not worth pursuing. He's learning to play the bagpipes ("the hardest thing I've ever played in my life") and also the concertina, an accordion-like instrument that requires a mastery of button pushing and timing. His other hobbies include the games he creates, including most recently a role-playing game called "Witness to the Execution."

Weinstein was eight or nine when his mother found an after-school computer-programming course at a community college in Worcester, Massachusetts, the small city where they were living. That was in the late 1970s, when learning to program meant punch cards and teletypes that hooked up to a hulking central computer invariably housed somewhere off the premises. He rattles off the model number of his first PC, a Radio Shack TRS-80, which looked like a toaster oven with a TV in it and a keyboard attached. His parents separated while he was in middle school and he moved with his father to rural Georgia just before his freshman year of high school. There, he got a Kaypro-II, which we used to call a "luggable"—an early laptop that felt like carrying bricks around in a heavy case. He went straight from his junior year to college at the University of Texas in Austin, where he studied computer science. He was sixteen when he began college—and nineteen when he stopped regularly attending classes. A part-time work-study job led to a full-time position at an on-campus lab that allowed him to work as a programmer in its artificial intelligence lab. "I basically dropped out of high school to go to college, and then I dropped out of college." His motivation for taking the job, he said, was less about impatience and more about finances and an opportunity to work with "some utterly brilliant people."

"I was fortunate," Weinstein said. "A lot of opportunities opened up for me because there was a community college around the corner teaching programming, and I was this middle-class kid with parents who could afford to buy computers back in the seventies and early eighties. That opened up a world of opportunities."

A backpacking trip in the Rockies made Weinstein think he'd rather live in Denver than Austin. Thus began the Long Strange Trip nature of Weinstein's journey. He worked for nearly four years at a library automation company in Denver and then satisfied a dream to get paid working in the video game world when he landed a job with a company called White Wolf Productions. Fifteen months later he moved to Charlottesville, Virginia, for a programmer job at a pioneer of the gaming world, Kesmai; two and a half years after that, he moved to the Raleigh, North Carolina area, where he worked for another big name in the gaming world, Red Storm, for nearly eight years. Weinstein declared all that moving around worth it. He was proud of all he had accomplished in the gaming world. He designed and built some core technologies for the Game Boy platform (memory management, text display). He built a set of networking tools optimized for game developers and had a hand in the creation and design of *Tom Clancy's Rainbow Six*, which, he told me with pride, is "still going strong twenty years later."

Weinstein confesses that he barely paid attention to security while working on games. "My relation to security at that point was being the problem and writing vulnerable code," he joked when I brought up the topic. Everything back then was about game speed, he explained: "When you fire a shot, you're sending a packet over the network. If there's a quarter-second delay? You're noticing that and you're frustrated." Building in security would only have slowed the game down. The mantra in the gaming world was engineering that was good enough. The idea was to make a great game and get it on the market as fast as possible. "The game industry is an unholy blend of the worst of tech and the worst of entertainment, and you as an employee are dealing with the worst of both worlds," he said.

The big shift in Weinstein's career came when he was in his midthirties. After twelve years in gaming, he took a job at Microsoft in security. Part of the decision was based on geography. He disliked the humid heat living in the Southeast, preferring a more temperate climate, even if it meant a lot of rain. The job also brought with it the challenge of helping the world's top software producer in the mid-2000s make its products safer. He had no security experience but that didn't seem to make a difference. "I went from working in the games industry, which has a massive talent oversupply, to a labor market equally distorted the other way." The world of games, he noted, has "thousands of talented people who would give everything they have to break in—so they can get underpaid and overworked." By contrast, those working security can never seem to find all the engineers and others they need to do the job. "There aren't enough skilled people for the roles," Weinstein said. "That's been true since I first got into security and true today given how the field continues to grow. Everybody has a website, half the things in your house are now connected to the internet."

The transition to security brought a sense of relief for Weinstein. In the past, he and his colleagues might have created a great game, but maybe the company had pushed it out before it was ready, or bungled the marketing, or simply had poor timing by releasing it into a marketplace where a book or a famous person's death can change the conversation for days. "There are plenty of great games out there that go nowhere," he said. "You need all these things to break in your favor and then almost none ever break through." A couple of cups of high-priced tea later, he confessed he had left games "because I was deeply burned out and I needed to make a significant switch to recover from that.

"In security, I have to be smart, I have to be clever," he continued. "But I don't have to create this great, unique game. I'm only trying to solve a technical problem, not pursue a solution at the intersection of a technical problem and an artistic problem."

Weinstein spent nearly eight years at Microsoft. He created a library of security tools based on an established technology called fuzz testing, which helps detect flaws in software by attacking an application with random and invalid data, and then trained people inside the company on using it. That included game developers inside the company's Xbox division, he said, "who had a habit of ignoring anything they don't want to hear with the argument 'You don't understand our business, we're different.' Well, I know that industry very well, and I was able to say you aren't the special snowflake you think you are." He spent his last couple of years with the company working for Bing as a senior software engineer in its search engine unit. "I spent a year at Bing working on a feature that I don't think I can talk about even to this day because I don't know that it ever shipped," Weinstein said.

Weinstein, feeling frustrated by this final assignment at Microsoft, jumped to Hewlett-Packard, which allowed him to expense an office near his home to avoid a daily commute into Seattle. There, he worked on a bug bounty program called the Zero Day Initiative until a Japan-based security company called Trend Micro took it over. "I used the acquisition as a time to look at my options," he said. "And the Google option was really compelling." At the beginning of 2016, he began as an information security engineer in its Android unit.

"When Google hires people, they have all the people who get hired in a given period of time, in a given region, do orientation together," he noted. Many of the people he interacted with were just out of school with their degrees and honors and he was already in his midforties, allowing him to appreciate the road that had gotten him there. He was working on Android, which is installed on more than two billion devices, on its Security Response and Review team. This is the group that responds when Google learns of a potential vulnerability in Android. Thirteen months later, he took over as an engineering manager of Android Security Assurance, where he runs a team of twelve people who analyze the various security issues reported to the company (or discovered internally), push out monthly patches, and handle ongoing long-term projects.

"I was a manager in 2000, 2001, at Red Storm, and I hated it," he said. He swore to himself he would never let himself be promoted to management ever again. Yet eventually he recognized that he was no longer the same person he was at thirty-one when he made that vow. "I spent the next fifteen years carefully looking at what I thought made a good manager because that's who I wanted to work for. And then I got to the point where it seemed like I knew what it took to be a good manager myself, and I thought it was the right thing to try." Engineers at Google are encouraged to nominate themselves if interested in moving into a managerial role, and that's what Weinstein did.

The question was what kind of boss he would be. He's endured the hands-on, meddling type who's always deep in everyone's code. But he saw himself more as coach or team leader—he guides and encourages more than passes down orders and imposing his will. "There are companies where my style just wouldn't work," he said. "At those companies

I simply would choose not to be a manager." He likes the work and likes the people he works with and likes, too, that he works on Seattle's Eastside, a not-too-unpleasant drive from his home. "A friend of mine had the rather interesting observation that I'm not the man I was ten years ago even if I still have pretty much all his stuff," Weinstein said. Google, he said, "feels like the right company at the right time."

Weinstein took a management training course, which made him more consciously think about the managers he had over the years and respected. "All of them had one core characteristic, although they were very, very different people: they prioritized the well-being of the people on their team over pretty much everything else." That's the kind of manager he strives to be—one who recognizes that it's not personal if a job isn't right for someone, even when that means headaches for you. "When you get right down to it, we're working together because our interests align." He knows that if he won the lottery tomorrow, he probably wouldn't be back at work the next day. "If someone says, 'Oh, I'm going to go somewhere else,' it's not a personal betrayal."

I could hear the management course leaking out occasionally, like when he told me, "You cannot 'you' hard enough to make this thing go away. It can't be done. You need other people." But it was also interesting to hear him process out loud the role he plays now as not just a member of the team but its leader. He quoted an article he had just read that pierced the myth that programming is sitting in your corner and writing code all day. "You're only able to do that as a junior engineer, and that's only because people senior to you are doing the rest of the work." Much of his day is spent in meetings—mainly with people on his team but also others throughout Android and other parts of Google. His job, he said, boils down to this: he has a set of problems that needs solving, and he has a set of people to help him solve them. "I need to find a way to get as much as I can done, while at the same time providing people with work they want to do and provide them with the challenges and opportunities for technical and career growth that they want and need.

"At some level you come to the realization that everything is about people—keeping them happy, keeping them productive," he said.

IN MAY 2018, WEINSTEIN took the stage at the local security conference called DefendCon. This was his chance, at the age of forty-eight, to share some of the wisdom he's gained from nearly three decades as a programmer and engineer, including thirteen in computer security. He called the speech "Building a Security Engineering Team," but it was really his opportunity to deflate tired old tropes he had been hearing for much of his career in tech. He began with a sampling of headlines that underscored that the demand for people interested in info-sec greatly outstrips the supply. (One example: "Fight Against Hackers Hurt by Huge Shortage of Cyber Workers.") But right away he was listing "fallacies" that get in the way of hiring good people.

Weinstein flashed a slide on the screen: ENTRY LEVEL IS NOT AN OPTION. That was fallacy number one and something he hears all the time in info-sec. "Companies will say, 'We can't afford to hire entry level; we need people who can hit the ground running,'" he said. But he had no security experience when he first went to work at Microsoft in his midthirties. "You can sit around and wait for the perfect unicorn, for the person who has all the skills you need for a role. But you're probably going to be unhappy because most of the time you'll be looking for that person for a long time." He wondered if sometimes that attitude wasn't a failure of management: surely a project can be broken down so there are tasks that can be accomplished by someone just entering the info-sec field. Rather than looking for the perfect background, he counseled, "Find people who want to solve problems."

Second and third on Weinstein's list of things a good hiring manager should never say: "The security mind-set is inborn, not teachable" and "Technical excellence requires an early start." These are corollaries to the idea that the only people worth pursuing in the info-sec world have been coding since they were in diapers, as Parisa Tabriz had put it. Almost everything is teachable, Weinstein said. "If you cannot teach something, you don't really understand it," Weinstein told the audience. "You may be able to do it, but you don't understand it." More important than looking for natural talent, he advised, is finding people who want to be engaged in your project. "You hear that people have a natural talent in X," he said. "What that really means is they found X engaging enough so they kept at it long enough until they got good at it. You have to be willing to be bad at something if you're ever going to be good at it." More important than skill level, he said, "is a curiosity to learn and a desire to get better.

"There's a common belief among people in the industry

that technical skill is all that matters. But I reject that," Weinstein said. "If you're technically very skilled but toxic to the people around you, they're better off removing you and replacing you with someone who is not toxic but maybe less skilled. You are not that special a snowflake. If you want to solve anything meaningful, you need to work with people."

There are people who at first glance seem perfect for a job. "They've got it in their bones," he said. "But someone who has been doing one job over and over, they know it well but maybe they don't want to do it anymore." Others are experts in a field because they've been trapped there for years and have had no choice. Those are the ones who really need help figuring out how to get unstuck. "I know people who are miserably unhappy in their job. I knew they were offered a new job but then I see them and they're like, 'Still at the old job.' And it's always the same when I ask them what happened. 'Oh, they gave me a big raise to stay.' And you know three months from now, they're still going to be miserably unhappy."

Who is he looking for when interviewing people for a position with him at Google? "I want to know someone really wants this job," he said. "The people I'm looking for want to learn, they want to do new things; they want a new challenge." One thing he watches out for, he said, are those who seem less interested in helping him with his job than simply looking for a job with the famous Google. "I'm looking for people who want to help me solve the problem I need solved." They don't even need the full tool set of talents he is seeking in the ideal candidate. "Given the choice between someone who has all the skills necessary to do this, but has done it before and doesn't want to do it again, and someone who has to be trained, but really wants to solve this problem, I will take the person who wants to solve the problem."

SITTING ACROSS FROM ME in the tea shop, Weinstein had advice for anyone signing up for the info-sec lifestyle. First and foremost, he advised, don't take the job too personally. "You have to care about it and be interested in solving problems, but for survival's sake you're going to have to recognize that things happen." Vulnerabilities and bugs are intrinsic to software, which is constantly morphing and growing. Occasionally, the bad guys cause trouble. "It's going to happen, and it's going to happen again," he said.

"You try and learn from it and make things better and make it harder for them to get in next time."

Weinstein brings up the defender's dilemma—the notion that an intruder needs to breach only one unprotected port, whereas the defender must successfully defend every possible entry point—billions of devices running Android and countless apps needing access to a phone's operating system. Weinstein and his colleagues can be successful every day for a year—but, at that scale, it's inevitable that Android ends up in the news because of the multiple Android vulnerabilities that are reported each year or a malicious app.

"Defense tends to attract people who want to play Atlas," Weinstein continued. "They want to put the heavens on their shoulders, lift it up, and protect it. The problem is, we know what happens if you put the world on your shoulders: you break. If you put yourself in a position where you must be perfect, you will break." His advice: "You can't internalize it when something goes wrong. You have to have both passion and dispassion." You have to care enough to solve the puzzle but also be able to dial down the intensity in a crisis. "You really need to understand the level of how bad something is, because there can be those things that aren't too bad and things so bad they're giving them a logo and a name."

Weinstein spools out more advice for those interested in info-sec as a career choice. "Another thing I would tell people is they always needs to be learning." In spring 2018 he gave a talk at RSA challenging the idea of failing privately to avoid looking foolish. "No one can be an expert in it all," he said. "If you don't know something, don't be afraid to ask questions. Go find senior people and ask: 'Could you explain this? I don't know what this is.'"

That's what he did—and he certainly does not regret his decision, almost a decade and a half ago, to move into security. "Two things I think I can say for certain," Weinstein said. "I don't think I'll ever be bored working security. And I don't think there will ever be a lack of demand in this field for the rest of my professional life." New software will be written, products updated, and new devices connected to a network. "It's not like we'll ever reach a point where we say 'Oh, we've solved this problem, this is settled technology.' Someone will find a workaround for your fix, and you'll go back and forth forever."

5

BUG HUNTERS

The story of why Patrick Wardle probably has few fans inside Apple starts with a nasty bit of malware called Fruitfly infecting Mac computers. "For more than a decade, an attacker was secretly hacking into Macs and turning on the webcam when the person wasn't there," Wardle explained. "One of his goals was to spy on children. Clearly, a really sick dude." Wardle, a regular onstage at Black Hat, DEF CON, and the other big security conferences, is an expert on vulnerabilities in the software that runs the Macintosh family of machines. "When I saw all the victims were in the U.S., I contacted the FBI and handed over all my research to them," he said, and then helped law enforcement find the digital footprints needed to track the attacker down.

Eventually, a suspect was arrested and Wardle, who had mentioned the vulnerability onstage at both Black

Hat and DEF CON, was free to talk about the experience without worrying that he was jeopardizing an ongoing investigation. "I gave this presentation and then got a message from someone at Apple giving me grief about the talk," Wardle said. His first instinct was to apologize. Had he inadvertently damaged the government's legal case or something that could compromise the privacy of the victims, many of whom were children? "I told them, 'I had the FBI vet my talk,' but it turned out it had nothing to do with that," he said. They were indignant that he was raising the subject at all. "There are all these articles saying Mac computers have been spying on children for the last decade, but they're worrying that me talking about it is giving them bad press, and we all know Apple hates bad press. They're like, 'The FBI has caught the guy, this is a contained threat; the average user is no longer at risk, so why are you even talking about it?'"

Normally, Wardle, thirty-five, is a low-key resident of Hawaii with a hang-loose attitude. Upbeat and a glass-half-full kind of guy, he's a surfer who posts pictures of pretty sunsets and uses "stoked" when expressing his excitement for something, or sometimes "super-stoked" if especially amped up about an experience. But he was decidedly not stoked talking to people from Apple after his speech. "They really pushed my buttons," he said. "I was like, 'Look, people need to know that there's these threats out there.' That was something I wasn't going to back down on." If anything, he felt his message was that much more relevant because it was directed at Apple devotees. "People who use Macs are often overconfident and naïve and I'd say it's because of Apple, which exudes this façade of impenetrability," Wardle said. "So people are like, 'Oh, we don't need antivirus on a Mac.' Which is part of the reason Mac users are getting infected with threats such as Fruitfly."

It wasn't personal with Apple. At least it hadn't started that way. When looking for his specialty, he chose the Mac, not because of any antipathy he felt toward Apple but because of his years working on top-secret projects for the U.S. government as a hacker for the National Security Agency (NSA). "I was mostly doing Windows-type stuff over there, so I didn't want to be talking publicly about Windows anything because I didn't want to cross any lines and inadvertently reveal any internal capabilities [of the NSA]. So I decided to focus on Mac security." He could still use the foundational skills he had learned working for the NSA, such as reverse engineering (deconstructing a finished product to the point where you can build it yourself), yet expose flaws on a platform he had never touched working for the government.

There was an advantage in a focus on Macs that Wardle wouldn't appreciate until he started finding vulnerabilities. This was in the early 2010s, when his employer at the time, a small security startup based in Silicon Valley, was eager to see him onstage at all the big hacker conferences, wearing the company T-shirt and winning them a mention in his official conference bio. "Talking about Macs when almost everyone else was talking about Windows machines was a little more provocative," he said. "It made what I had to say more unique when I was talking to the media or doing presentations." There are many more malicious programs aimed at Windows computers than target Macs, in no small part because there are far more Windows-based machines in the world than Macs. Yet that's not to say Wardle was ever at a loss for things to talk about. By his calculations, he's spoken five times at DEF CON and given several more speeches at Black Hat. There have been another four or so talks at RSA and appearances at a range of other security conferences, including Hack in the Box, ShmooCon, ZeroNight, and PHDays in Russia. In almost every speech,

Wardle has spoken at length about vulnerabilities in Macs. "Not even iOS," he said, referring to the operating system on Apple's iPhones and iPads. "Basically just the Mac."

His decision, in other words, to become a guy who "collects macOS malware," as his Black Hat bio describes him, in his spare time has proven a sage one. But it's also meant a different relationship with Apple than bug hunters who have chosen to focus on Windows. "Microsoft has responded in the emotionally mature way and really embraced this idea that any code is gonna have bugs and vulnerabilities," Wardle said. "They have really good bug bounty programs and work with hackers and researchers." Apple, in contrast, he said, "seems to be content in their walled garden. They exude this hubris like, 'We do everything right, we're more secure.'" Yet that attitude has worked in Wardle's favor. "Their products are just as hackable as Windows'. So when I tell people, 'Look, I can hack this Mac in ten seconds,' well, people really pay attention."

WARDLE WAS NOT THE kid already tapping at a computer while still in diapers. He grew up in a deeply religious household without a television, let alone a computer, in a small town in Pennsylvania a long way from either Pittsburgh or Philadelphia. "I was brought up kind of on the poor end of things," he said, and yet still described his earliest years as "idyllic." Despite tight finances, his parents sent him to a private religious school he described as "focused on instilling a love of learning and curiosity that I think has really served me well." By the eighth grade, however, his family had moved to Connecticut and he attended the local public school. "That's when my life took an interesting turn," Wardle said.

His family was growing increasingly religious, he explained, and he was not. "I actually moved out when I was fifteen." He lived with a family friend until his sixteenth birthday, which is when he decided to move into his own apartment. "That's when my parents said, 'Okay, well, if this is something you truly have to do.' And they gave me $500 and basically said 'Good luck.' So at an early age I literally had to grow up quickly." In retrospect, Wardle said, he viewed the independence his parents granted him as a gift.

Life then, as he described it, could be grim. His apartment had a fireplace but no heat, which meant he was constantly feeling cold during the winter. He lived on food stamps and what he described as a "very, very minimal income." He lucked into a job with a moving company that paid him $10 an hour, which was a lot for a high schooler. "But I still sometimes had to take time off from school to make extra money so I could pay rent, put gas in my car, pay for everything," he said. That car was a "piece of shit Mercury Topaz" that got him from point A to point B— most of the time. Eventually, he got a maintenance job at a local YMCA camp. The work could be thankless ("cleaning toilets and painting and that kind of stuff") but the perks priceless: "I'd go there after school to work, and they let me stay for dinner, so I knew I was getting at least one good meal a day." Food stamps are "super embarrassing," he said, when you attend an "upper-middle-class Connecticut high school where parents buy their kids brand-new cars for their sixteenth birthday. It's hard to be one of the cool kids when you're on school lunch vouchers and food stamps." But he was thankful to be attending a well-funded school that was strong on academics. Despite everything, he got good grades and graduated in what he described as the top 5 percent of his class. "I was always that kid who picks up things really fast," he noted.

His status as a kid living on the economic fringes would prove a huge plus when applying to college. Scholarship offers were plentiful, as was financial aid. Wardle's main criterion was making sure he ended up somewhere warm. "I was thinking Florida or maybe California but then I was like, 'Wait, there are colleges in Hawaii,'" he said. The seventeen-year-old who was living on his own and making up his own mind decided he'd go to school at the University of Hawaii in Honolulu. Wardle, ever the optimist, declared himself "super-stoked that these hardships really guided me to where I am today. I have nothing but gratefulness that the universe, in its infinite wisdom or random coincidence, got me where I am."

The first time Wardle remembers touching a computer was a machine his parents had bought for his older brother, a cheap Tandy from Radio Shack, shortly before he moved out of the house. He traveled with that same brother to a computer show in Hartford, the big city nearest to where they lived. There, they bought the parts to assemble their own machine, which Wardle dubbed "a rite of passage for people of a certain age who were interested in computers." His first hack was in high school and involved a programmable Texas Instruments calculator that he had saved up to buy. Calculators were permitted during tests for simple calculations only but Wardle designed a simple workaround. "I'd write a program with an innocuous front-end that might tell what day of the week it would be in three months, that kind of thing," he said. "But if you typed in certain key sequences, it would take you to the secret menu that would let you calculate derivatives and integrals and things like that." He was no better in math or science than other subjects, "and certainly no math prodigy." He had no idea what he might want to do after college. Yet it was perhaps inevitable that he would major in computer science wherever he went to school.

His first couple of years as a computer science major proved disappointing. He was learning the basics, which he described as "some programming, some database work, and OS [operating system] internals," but felt bored. The viruses, worms, and backdoor Trojan horses making headlines in the early 2000s were what interested him, yet in school "we were learning nothing related to hacking or computer security." On his own, he started following the sites that reported on the viruses and other attacks that were plaguing websites and businesses then, as the world was becoming more interconnected. To the extent he had any affiliation with computers, it seemed it was a fascination with the malware and other contagions out in the world. "I would read about this stuff on the weekends and follow the tutorials online to see how it worked," he said. "I would read the virus writers online. I got really interested in reverse engineering, which really wasn't taught in my classes."

Wardle credits a work-study job with changing his life. The price of being the poor kid at school was a job working the front desk at the computer center to help earn his tuition and room and board. That led to what he described as "my first real programming job" when a university staffer invited him to join a team designing a web-based program that allowed students to log in and track their coursework and check on how many credits they had earned. "He took a big gamble on me," Wardle said. "At the time, I wasn't much of a programmer. I really blossomed under his guidance." The computer center is also where he saw a flyer taped to a door announcing that the NSA would be on campus the next day. Wardle had no idea the acronym stood for the National Security Agency, though insiders crack that it really means No Such Agency because it's the kind of deep-state organization that leaves few fingerprints on what it touches. "I googled them and was like, 'Oh, wow, they look like they do really cool stuff.'"

The presentation the next day was a low-key affair. These days a gathering like that might even draw protests, but back in the early 2000s there was only a recruiter standing at the front of a room of students, trying to rev them up about fighting the bad guys in cyberspace. "He described what the NSA did as far as breaking codes and computer-hacking stuff," said Wardle, who was intrigued to the point that he met one-on-one with the recruiter.

The man's first question was whether he was a computer science major. When Wardle answered yes, the man explained that they had a strict drug policy. "Do you think you could pass a polygraph test?" the man asked. "Yeah, I think so," Wardle responded half-heartedly, and yet suddenly he felt as if he was in the middle of an impromptu job interview of the kind you hear about in Silicon Valley. "He's asking me these silly questions like, 'Why are man-hole covers round?'" That Wardle had a perfect response to the manhole question is almost beside the point in his telling of the story. ("Luckily, I could figure out the answer for that, so that when you turn them on their side they don't fall in, because if they were square you'd have the hypotenuse, blah blah blah.") He was a computer science major who had stayed away from drugs because he had wanted to prove something to his parents—and now he was viewed as a strong candidate for top-secret government work. He filled out the standard government form that anyone seeking security clearance must, asking the applicant to list places they've lived and people they've associated with. The next step was a trip to the NSA's headquarters just outside Baltimore, where he submitted to a lie detector test about drug use and other aspects of his past. "They strapped me to a chair, asked me all sorts of questions, and that was that," he said. He was in.

Wardle began working as a NSA intern in the summer of 2004. He was given a semester off and paid a comfortable stipend. His first assignment was in cryptography, which is the art of scrambling data so it can't be read by others. Cryptography typically involves advanced math, "and math is not my forte, but it was a good intro to the agency and what it does," he said. "They really teach you, offering training, and then mentor you."

One semester at the agency stretched into two and included a second summer. He moved to what he called the Maliciotus Code Analysis branch, where, even as a lowly intern, he was "seeing just incredibly sophisticated malware in the wild." A malicious program would hit a server at the Department of Defense or some other branch of government and it was his unit's job to study the offending software. "I was a young computer security researcher," he said. "That's the kind of stuff we geek out on." Wardle was able to reverse engineer a few of the "new samples," as he labeled them, that came into the office. That led to him writing papers that were read by higher-ups in the Defense Department.

His third and final posting inside the NSA had him moving from what he called the "defensive side of the house" to the "offense side." "The NSA has two missions," Wardle explained. One is defensive and includes cryptography and malware analysis. The other is offense, a mission that lives largely under the auspices of the spy agency's Tailored Access Operations hacking team. He'd be assigned a target, and then instructed to do what he could to break into a system and take control of it. "Working for the hacking branch, basically doing vulnerability research, was this incredibly empowering, I would say almost addictive, experience," he said.

"That's the pivotal, foundational experience that really got me where I am today. Because if you're interested in computer hacking, there's very few places where you can actually get practical hands-on exposure."

Wardle returned to Honolulu but was more or less done with the classroom. A professor of his was doing side work for NASA and roped him into a project that had him working as an intern with the space agency's autonomous software division. There he worked on safety systems for both the space shuttle and Mars rover, which could be described as a self-driving minicar designed to propel itself across the surface of a faraway planet. "Basically, we had to ensure that the code wouldn't deadlock and freeze up while this thing is on Mars," Wardle said.

Wardle faced a dilemma when he graduated from the University of Hawaii in 2005. One possibility had him continuing to work with NASA. "I don't want to say I was the dumbest person there, but I literally was working with rocket scientists," he said. "The people there were just incredibly, incredibly bright." There seemed to be a job waiting for him at NASA but the lure of the NSA proved too great. He was offered a job with the Tailored Access Operations, on the offense side, which had been his favorite posting during his year there. "I guess I had done good work because they were stoked to have me back."

In many ways, the NSA proved a dream job. The work was always interesting and the perks nothing short of amazing. Wardle enrolled in the agency's "20/20 program." That let him work only twenty hours a week and attend graduate school (the "other" twenty hours, even if neither graduate school nor security work lends itself to a strict forty-hour week) while pulling down a full-time salary. He took classes at Johns Hopkins, which was just twenty miles from the NSA. He earned a dual master's in computer science and information security but also questioned the intrinsic worth of the diploma he was issued. "Especially for computer hacking, the hands-on experience is way more important than any school learning you're getting," he said. "Everything I learned was from working at the NSA and reading stuff outside of class assignments." At least the government was picking up the tab.

A sense of patriotic duty added to Wardle's good feeling about the work he was doing. "I got to college right around the time of 9/11 and there was something very inspiring about doing something to help my country," he said. The government had provided him with food stamps when he was in high school and financial aid to attend college. It felt satisfying to be able to give back, especially after the country was attacked. "Regardless of people's political views, we were doing antiterrorism work. We were directly assisting national security." He also felt good about most of the people he encountered while working inside the spy agency. "I saw a lot of hardworking, everyday Americans who really believe in what they're doing. The vast majority of them are very good, hardworking, passionate people. It felt incredibly fulfilling going into work each day." Wardle still keeps on his desk an award his team won in 2007 after "we pulled off an epic hack and avoided an international incident. Nothing beats the thrill of being an NSA hacker."

Yet the job also had its frustrations. Accepting practically any interested computer science student who was able to pass a drug test, as he suspected, isn't the most inspiring way to build a staff. "A lot of the people we had coming in just couldn't cut it technically, and the NSA doesn't fire people unless you're Snowden leaking secrets," Wardle said, referring to Edward Snowden, who copied and leaked classified information from the NSA in 2013. There were also the hassles that come from working inside a giant government bureaucracy. They'd have sign-off from the director of the NSA himself yet the middle managers who hadn't been briefed would feel slighted and do whatever they could to thwart their efforts. A small team of crackerjack analysts, operatives, and other hackers would have been assembled and ready to hit what he described as a "hard target" but then nothing in government, it seemed, was that simple. Permission would be denied, turf declared, egos clashing with other egos. "The challenges we ran into were rarely technical in nature," he said. In the fall of 2008, after nearly three years on the job, or four if counting his yearlong internship, he gave notice at a dream gig but one he was ready to leave.

THE TRANSITION FROM THE NSA to the regular world can be a hard one. "People inside the NSA knew I was good at computer security but the weird thing is you really can't talk about anything you did there," said Charlie Miller, who left the NSA at around the time Wardle first showed up as an intern. "It's kind of hard to land that first job out of government when you can't even prove you know anything about computer security." Wardle's solution, along with that of four colleagues he met while working at the NSA, was to create their own company. Called Vulnerability Research Labs, they rented space in a building only a few miles from their old offices. Wardle took the title of chief scientist in this small consultancy promising to help organizations protect themselves from the same computer attacks they were researching while working for the government.

Wardle could offer little in the way of specifics when talking about his time with the NSA, and he's similarly limited in what he can say about his work for Vulnerability Research. "You know how government agencies sometimes need capabilities and they turn to companies in the private sector to help them with that?" Wardle said. Vulnerability Research ended up being one of those companies. Instead, he described the work life of pretty much any security researcher, if not most ethical hackers. "There's a lot of time when you're just sitting in front of the computer, reading technical documents, or reverse engineering. A lot of it is nose-to-the-grindstone work." He wrote research papers when he wasn't doing work for clients or cocreating what he called a "heuristic-based malware framework"—in English, a way clients could better understand a threat on their own. "I don't think I ever found it boring, but let's just say it's not always exciting," Wardle commented. "It may seem different from the outside but the hacker's life is not especially sexy."

The job got stressful when "things went sideways," as Wardle put it—a regular part of life in a business that tracked and captured new bugs unleashed in the ecosystem. "You constantly are like, 'Hey, if I don't get this done, or if I don't get this working, or I don't get access to this target, what are the consequences of that?'" Wardle said. "The biggest stress of the job is that the work never ends. Everything is a priority and it needs to be done now." The stakes might not have been as great as when he worked for the NSA, "where, say, you're trying to hack into a terrorist network." But then he was still helping the government do intelligence work and fight attacks, even if more in an auxiliary role.

With hard work came success. Barely two years after the five colleagues ventured out on their own, Vulnerability Research was bought by a much larger company called Computer Sciences Corporation (itself now part of a U.S.-based multinational called DXC Technology). For Wardle, that may have been good news for his net worth but it doomed any possibility that Vulnerability Research would serve as a longtime home. "Things kind of started to change," he said. "They were this publicly traded company interested in quarterly profits and meeting numbers. We were a research-minded organization." The research Wardle and his partners were doing could take months to pay off, if not a year or more. "I decided it was time to leave."

Wardle moved back to Hawaii, a place he had never really wanted to leave. He worked remotely for Computer Sciences Corporation while he and his wife, Riane, who he had met while attending the University of Hawaii, looked to put down roots. That would prove Wardle's big moment of fame: The couple's quest in 2014 to find the perfect home in Maui is an episode of the long-running HGTV television show *House Hunters*. An episode guide captures the tension: "Riane wants a funky home with good vibes and lots of land." The ever-practical Patrick is seeking a good investment. An ocean view is a priority for both, except "Riane is terrified of [t]sunamis and wants her new home as high as possible."[*] The episode ends with them finding the perfect home with an ocean view but located high on a hill. That's where Wardle set up shop.

"One of the reasons I love it here is people really value health and happiness over money. The life out here is

---

[*] *House Hunters*, Season 62, Episode 3, "Mainlanders Settle Down in Maui," https://www.hgtv.com/shows/house-hunters/episodes/mainlanders -settle-down-in-maui.

pretty low stress. If you drive a fancy car, people almost look down on you, like, 'Why are you wasting money on that? That's silly.'" He experienced the opposite in his early twenties, when he was living outside Washington, D.C., and bought a black BMW because that's what he thought he needed to do now that he was earning good money. He cringes looking back on that aspect of his younger self. "Maui is the complete opposite. It really has influenced my mentality on how I approach things." These days he surfs a lot, does yoga, travels, and takes on interesting projects as they present themselves: some for money and some more for himself.

In 2013, Wardle became employee number six at a new security firm in the San Francisco Bay Area founded by a pair of former NSA agents. Called Synack, its selling point would be a network of freelance security hackers based in more than fifty countries constantly checking for vulnerabilities and security problems. "I basically grew their research team," he said, and also did what he could to raise its public profile. His macOS research had no relation to Synack's core business, but his bosses back in San Francisco were happy with the attention. "Because they were this small startup, they needed some assistance with brand awareness," Wardle said. "They were cool with me talking about it. So I started talking at all these big computer security conferences like Black Hat and RSA. I would say that's when my public security career took off."

YOU CAN CALL WARDLE an ethical hacker—or, more formally, a security researcher. But he's many other things as well: a speaker, a tool maker (the digital kind), an entrepreneur, a conference impresario, an expert. He's quoted regularly in the *New York Times* and *Wired* and has appeared on both CNN and MSNBC. He blogs about Mac vulnerabilities as often as several times a month, and reports the occasional bug to Apple. I googled "Mac security researcher" at the end of 2018 and the first three hits were about Wardle.

His security researcher bona fides are rock-solid. In 2018, Wardle took the stage at the Flamingo Las Vegas for DEF CON 26 to unveil his latest discovery: a vulnerability that let him gain access to the Mac operating system and full control over a machine. Two years earlier, Wardle was all over the media (from industry trade sites such as *Slashdot* and *Motherboard* to the *New York Post*) talking about Shazam, the popular app that can identify a song in just a few seconds. After receiving a tip from a source, Wardle reverse engineered Shazam and discovered that it was *always* listening: Its microphone remains engaged even when the application is turned off. (Shazam confirmed what Wardle had found but described it as a feature, not a bug. In a statement the company provided the tech website *The Register* in 2016: "If the mic wasn't left on, it would take the app longer to both initialize the mic and then start buffering audio," which the company declared "a poor user experience.")[*]

In 2015, Wardle created Objective-See, which is a word-play on what had long been Apple's primary programming language, Objective-C, until the introduction of Swift in 2014. Over the years, he has created tools and utilities to fight Mac malware (for instance, a simple program that issues an alert when a webcam has been turned on); Objective-See is the private venture he has created for sharing it all. "They're one hundred percent free," he said. "There are no ads built into them, no limited functionality to get you to upgrade to

---

[*] John Leyden, "Shhh! Shazam Is Always Listening—Even When It's Been Switched 'Off,'" *The Register*, November 15, 2016, https://www.the register.co.uk/2016/11/15/shazam_listening/.

a premium version. I'm a firm believer in end-user tools that help people protect their computers." He set up a page for those who wanted to pay a little every month for his service, almost like a monthly tip for his contributions. As of fall 2018, over a thousand people were donating $6,000 a month for a suite of free Mac security products.

"The older I get, the more I learn that if you do something for altruistic reasons, there can be a huge financial upside anyway," he said. "The tools are free but people are so super-stoked that they want to support me, so now there's a significant amount of revenue coming in."

The tools are also at the center of his latest business. Wardle left Synack at the start of 2018 to create a new company he cofounded with the friends from Vulnerability Research. Called Digita Security, they are taking the tools Wardle designed for individuals and selling them as a single product for large organizations that want to better protect themselves from malware in the Mac universe. "If there's a big company using something I've created, I have no problem selling that," Wardle said.

Things have gotten better with Apple. The company at least seems to have grown accustomed to the likes of Wardle and other security researchers. In 2016, Apple announced its first bug bounty program, long after most other big tech firms. But they limited participation to those who had been invited into the program, a group that didn't include Wardle. Wardle focused on Macs, and though that franchise is important to Apple, it's not nearly as central to the company's continued success as the iPhone. As of early 2019, that was still the only focus of Apple's bug bounty program: the iPhone iOS. The reason why, a spokesperson for Apple's security team explained, were the conversations with their counterparts at Microsoft, Google, and other big tech companies when Apple was first considering a bug bounty program. "They advised us to go slow," he said. Don't announce a program until you have the infrastructure in place to handle the logistics of evaluating a bug report and deciding how much that information might be worth. "They told us, 'Don't let it mushroom into something you can't handle. We want to give any program we start the attention it deserves.'" It was a matter of resources, in other words: the people in place to deal with any hackers who come to them saying they've found a security issue related to an Apple product. Billy Rios headed up such a program at Google between 2010 and 2013 and said he had all of nine engineers working for him to handle "any security issue relating to any Google product from someone outside Google." It seemed a lack of priority for a company that reported $59 billion in profits in 2018.

Still, Wardle was expected to report whatever he found to its engineers before telling the wider world about what he had found, though he receives no money for any vulnerability he brings to Apple. By this point, he knows some of its security people and they know him. They'll chat at security conferences, and Wardle has even gotten in the habit of sitting down with a couple of them when he's in Silicon Valley, which Wardle appreciates even as he mistrusts the corporate overlords who make policy for the company. Apple even sent a member of its security team to Hawaii last November to a conference he was hosting. It was called Objective by the Sea, and Wardle dubbed it the world's first Mac security conference. Among his goals was drawing local high schoolers to what he hopes will be an annual affair. "We want to show that you don't have to be this math prodigy, that if you're willing to work hard, this [the computer security field] can be this incredible, incredible career that can be fulfilling and challenging and pay the bills while you're helping out other people." And, Wardle added, "still have enough time to surf."

At this point, Wardle's various worlds have merged. Finally, his interest in finding vulnerabilities in macOS has synced with the rest of his work life. He still travels the world giving talks about security, except now his badge identifies him as Patrick from Digita rather than Patrick from Synack, and he doesn't have to feel weird that what he is talking about has nothing to do with the company that pays him a salary.

"I feel like I have this incredible dream job," Wardle said. "I'm able to talk at all these computer security conferences all over the world and they're paying for your travel and your hotel. I feel like I've unlocked the secret of how to travel the world for free. I go to conferences in Dubai, India, South America, Australia." The following day, he told me, he was off to Asia. "I'm giving a talk at a conference in the Philippines, but I'm going early so I can go scuba diving. It's amazing."

Wardle is once again single. "Riane and I amicably went our separate ways in 2015," he said. A year or two later, he was in Moscow for a security conference and went on a Tinder date with a woman who, it turned out, worked for Russia's Ministry of Foreign Affairs. That got him thinking about what some in the info-sec world call an "evil maid" attack: someone gaining unauthorized physical access to a machine and inserting an undetectable trapdoor for later use. He had nothing to worry about. The always security conscious former NSA staffer had been cautious enough to bring only a "burner" laptop with him—a machine stripped of any personal information. But it gave him the idea for what he called the Do Not Disturb app, which, when switched on, sends the user a notification if someone opens the lid—and snaps a picture, if that's the user's desire, or shuts down the computer, or surreptitiously records the screen activity.

In 2018, Wardle was again in Moscow for a conference. So, too, was Vice News, which was recording an episode about Russian hacking. The challenge they gave Wardle: Hack our producer and we'll put you on TV—on HBO. "And I was like, 'Say no more.'" Challenge accepted. He and a local hacker friend created their own "guest" network at the producer's hotel, which fooled her into giving them her room number. They obtained a key to her room through a bit of social engineering (the other hacker's wife called the hotel pretending to be the producer and asked that they give her coworker, Patrick, a key so he could pick up the important document she supposedly had left behind). Using that key, they set up hidden cameras in the room to capture the producer's usernames, passwords, and the combination to the room safe if she used it. "We got access to her laptop, her Instagram, her Twitter, her webcam," Wardle said. Using her credit card number, they also bought her a small Russian flag as a souvenir.

"In what other job is it like, 'Okay, go to Russia, hack someone you won't get in trouble for hacking, and then you'll be on HBO?' It's like this dream, dream job."

Yet even without these moments of fame and adventure, Wardle would have only positive things to say about security as a field. "People ask, 'What's a career where I can make a ton of money?' Well, this is one of those careers," Wardle said. The ethical hacker can choose to work daunting hours or opt for more of a 9:30 a.m. to 6:00 p.m. gig and still earn in the six figures. He or she can travel or never leave town.

"Computer security is this field with amazing job security that gives you lots of time to work remotely, and there's something new every day," he said. "For me it's something I love to do and that I'm passionate about. It's something I'm good at. It's something the world needs, and it's something that compensates you really well financially. So for me it checks all the boxes: this incredible, incredible career that's fulfilling, challenging, pays the bills, *and* you're helping other people. When you can check off all four of those boxes, you're fulfilled."

6

PRODIGY

Allison Wong was in third grade the first time she touched a computer. "It changed my life," she said. At first a video game popular in the 1980s called *The Oregon Trail* was her obsession, but quickly she was going deeper into the machine. Wong, who grew up in Houston, was programming on DOS-based (the precursor to Windows) machines by the time she was in sixth grade. That was around the time an Apple computer hooked up to the internet showed up in her living room. That was in 1991, before the average family owned a computer, let alone had internet access at home. But Wong's father was in the military and often away for months at a time. "It's the way we all stayed in touch," said Wong, now thirty-eight.

The internet exposed Wong to online bulletin boards, which were an early iteration of the chat rooms that followed. These sites were no more visually appealing than computer code on a screen but Wong spent hours reading postings on these web-based group hangouts. She was at home, her nails painted black, listening to heavy metal or techno, lurking on one of several bulletin boards she frequented, soaking up knowledge about programming and computers. Online, she was ChinaWhite because, she said, "I'm half Chinese and half white." Only later did she learn that "China White" was slang for heroin. "I was too young to have a clue," she said. She was a self-described "super-nerd" who eventually started participating in these online back-and-forths with fellow programmers from around the world. All of them seemed to be using Linux, a new operating system that offered a range of applications useful for anyone programming on a home computer. By fourteen, she had built her own Linux-based computer.

She was still a high schooler when an internet service provider (ISP) hired Wong to do tech support after school and on weekends. For Wong, the job "was less about the money than the free bandwidth." She wanted free, unlimited internet access in exchange for a job she found easy to do. "This was like 1996," she said. "People were getting their Gateway and Dell computers and were really excited to get on the internet but clueless. I had people to whom I'd say 'mouse' and they thought I was talking about a pest running around the house."

COLLEGE WAS ALWAYS THE plan. As a high school senior, Wong interviewed for a local scholarship program run by Lockheed Martin, the giant space and defense contractor. But she was also a working-class kid who had nothing going for her but raw talent. She told me when we met in San Francisco in the fall of 2018 that it went to someone else. Her consolation prize, she told me with a good-natured smile, despite the obvious sting of her story, was a job for Lockheed working at NASA's Johnson Space Center in Houston. She would start at the University of Houston in fall 1998 but already college seemed almost beside the point. That summer she started work as a "system administrator" for the space shuttle program. She had a newly minted high school diploma yet was working on systems that ensured that the "pyrotechnic initiators"—small explosive devices that ring the shuttle before takeoff—ignite simultaneously to ensure its release into space. Her salary, she said, $40,000 a year, matched her parents' combined income. "People teased me about being so young. They'd leave *Seventeen* magazine on my desk as a joke." Once school started, she'd work after classes late into the night, and devote a lot of every weekend to the job. So inspiring did she find the work that she briefly considered chucking computers as a career choice. "I was literally working with rocket scientists and thought maybe that's what I'd like to be when I grow up."

The job at NASA lasted around a year. But rather than going back to being a full-time student for whom a job might be part-time food server at one of the dorm cafeterias, she took a job with another ISP, complete with health benefits and a 401(k). This time she wouldn't work as a tech support rep but serve as the company's network administrator. That meant the nineteen-year-old Wong was responsible for software upgrades and maintenance of the network. She was also responsible if it crashed or experienced a breach. This was in the late 1990s, before most people had cell phones, and so it was a pager that was her constant companion. "My pager would go off at two a.m. and I'd have to go in and reboot the system," she said. Or an issue with an ISP server would mean leaving a class partway through a lecture. "My parents weren't in a financial place to support me," she noted. "I had to work."

It seemed inevitable that Wong would drop out. School was standing in the way of her earning power and not really teaching her much that seemed relevant to her work as a systems administrator. She was learning to program in C, the dominant computer language at the time, but "that really didn't have any application to what I was doing in the real world," Wong said. For the job at the ISP she was usually working in Perl or Python, two other programming languages. Those she picked up reading guides (*Learning Perl*, the *Python Cookbook*) sold by O'Reilly Media, a popular publisher specializing in technology books. She was also teaching herself security—something else that never came up in her coursework. She taught herself to install firewalls throughout her system and found off-the-rack tools for pen testing her own network. "Everything I've done in cybersecurity flowed from there," she said.

The shift to computer security was solidified during her junior year, when Wong left the ISP for a full-time job with a Dallas-based security firm. This new posting had her traveling the world as a consultant. Her first assignment was a long-term one that meant moving temporarily to Europe to work for a client there. "I told myself I'd just be taking a couple of semesters off," she said. Wong was just twenty when she moved to Europe. She was an international security consultant working for a huge global player, installing firewalls and other security measures in the data centers it operated around the globe. "I was the one overseeing everything," Wong said. "It was me traveling the world, making sure everything got done right." While in Mexico attending a security conference, she met a Ukrainian-born cyberpunk who would become her boyfriend and, eventually, fiancé, though the two would never marry. She was in love. She was earning what she described as a "six-figure salary." And she was taking to the excitement of the far-flung, itinerant life she was leading. She never returned to the University of Houston. "I really enjoyed international consulting," she said. "I thought that's where I wanted to be."

September 11 put a kink in those plans. Wong was wrapping up the firewall project by the time terrorists struck the U.S. in 2001. "I think we all agreed that maybe it would be best if we finished the job from home," she said. Back in Dallas, she let herself be wooed by a rival security consulting firm in town. She'd work sales at this job because she wanted the bigger paycheck. And who knew, maybe she'd enjoy selling clients on the firm's services rather than doing the jobs herself. That job lasted maybe six months. "I really missed the technical side," she said.

Wong stayed in her next posting for just over five years. Her initial employer was Citadel Security Software, which Wong described as in the "vulnerability management" business: the firm would scan networks looking for gaps in its architecture and then provide the necessary countermeasures. Among her clients: the Department of Defense. Her job was to handle the installations that the company sold to the government. "I got to go to every military base in the U.S., as well as every VA [Veterans Affairs] hospital," Wong said. That was another job she really enjoyed. "In a way, I was a security engineer for the Department of Defense. I helped them understand what their needs were and then helped them architect the right security solution. I also did their trainings."

McAfee, a giant of the security software world, bought Citadel in 2006, a few years into Wong's tenure with the firm. Then, in her midtwenties, she was a senior security engineer overseeing the creation of new products and working with others in the company to integrate any new offerings into the packages that the company sold both to individual users and large corporations. Maybe the biggest challenge in her new role was the requirement that she speak multiple languages with the wide constellation of people

now in her orbit, including fellow technologists, people on
the business side of the company, the media, and customers.
"It was a great experience," she said.

Wong's time at McAfee came to an end when she met
the man she would eventually marry. He, too, worked at
McAfee, and she didn't want to work at the same company
as her spouse. Instead, she would work at McAfee's main
competitor, Symantec, where she would spend another
five or so years. Those first couple of years had her again
working in more of a customer-facing role. "Symantec was
very good for me," she said. "I got to work as a security
architect. Working with customers, understanding their
requirements." Her customers included Google and eBay,
and also Visa, which presented an interesting challenge: a
business tied to millions of stores and restaurants around
the globe but with no real control over the security used
when one of its retail customers confirms a charge. Her
mistake was transferring to a product manager role.
That led to her exit from Symantec. She had helped to
conceive and oversee the building of a new product she
had been excited about—and then watched in frustration
as the company bungled the marketing and rolled out
another product that effectively killed her own. "I felt

emotionally attached to this product and frustrated that it didn't make it."

Wong's next stop was a security company called Websense, which Raytheon, the giant weapons maker, bought and renamed Forcepoint. There Wong worked as a "consulting systems engineer," which meant she was responsible for helping customers anywhere in North America deploy the network security appliances the company sold. It was consultants like Wong who recommended that clients buy these products and then they charged as well for the implementation and maintenance required. "I enjoyed it but the company wasn't really evolving after the acquisition," she said. She was given shares in Websense, which she was able to cash out after the Raytheon buyout. "I made some money so I just left."

Wong didn't rest for long. Soon she was working for FireEye, based in Silicon Valley and a giant of the security industry. The publicly traded FireEye is really two companies merged into one. The original FireEye sold security tools, management systems, and software, along with its consulting services. It went public in September 2013—and by December of that year, the company spent over $1 billion of its newfound stock market gains to buy

Mandiant, a top player in Angela Gunn's world of firefighters and incident response. These days FireEye has a lot of analysts looking for potential threats and chasing down malware and the black hats behind it. Its CEO (a former air force officer and Mandiant's founder) has testified before the U.S. Senate about Russian hackers and Facebook, and its executives are frequently quoted in the media, whether the topic is state-sponsored digital attacks (FireEye is famous for revealing connections between attacks out of China and a unit of its People's Liberation Army) or the latest major breach that has hit yet another large, brand-name, once-trusted company.

Wong joined the Mandiant side of FireEye in 2014, shortly after the acquisition. She seemed to enjoy the work, sounding much like Gunn when talking about what amounted to a three-year stint in incident response. "There's an excitement when you're in the war room with the chief security officer, figuring out in real time what happened, helping them figure out what they need to do and gathering up forensics," she said. The flip side of the job, though, was the tensions inherent to a job that invariably meant showing up when people were at their worst. Occasionally she would be screamed at by someone believing that a product FireEye had sold them should have stopped the breach. "Being in the trenches as a firefighter was probably the most stressful" of all her roles, Wong said.

She was also a little more than fed up working somewhere that was overwhelmingly male. Data provided by FireEye showed that roughly 10 percent of its engineers were women in 2014, or 20 percent if including anyone with technical expertise—better numbers than many in the industry. Yet to Wong it still felt "very much a boy's club." It was then that she decided to get more involved with Women in Technology and other efforts to bring more women into the industry. "It's a very small world for women in cybersecurity," she said, and added, with a laugh, "I'd like some company."

IT WAS A BEAUTIFUL, sunny Friday afternoon in San Francisco when I met Wong in October 2018. She was dressed entirely in black. Wong, who has a round face and dark black hair, greeted me with a firm handshake and a broad, easy smile—a security engineer who, from almost the start of her career, had been interacting with clients and higher-ups inside the companies she worked. We squeeze around a table at a small coffee stall outside San Francisco's Ferry Building at the foot of Market Street. The Blue Angels—daredevil pilots who dazzle onlookers with their in-air acrobatics—are in town for Fleet Week, which means fighter jets roaring above us as we talk. There are moments when Wong was practically yelling to be heard.

Wong seemed happy as she talked about her career dating back to her days working tech support as a teenager in Houston. "The quality of life a career in computer security lets you afford is very good," she said. Defense work pays especially well, she said. Her work at a security firm like McAfee or Symantec meant bringing home somewhere around $300,000 a year, and various jobs she's held came with big bonuses in the form of stock options. These days she lives in a house in Alameda, a small island community located across the bay from San Francisco. There she lives with her husband and their baby, who was born six months earlier. She's also self-employed for the first time in her life. In 2016, while still working at FireEye, Wong and her husband, Afonso Infante, began batting around the idea of starting their own security firm. At the beginning of 2018, they quit their jobs to see if they could make a go of their idea.

The company is called Suavei, which comes from the

Portuguese (Infante's nationality) for "soft." Wong explained the name for me during our coffee: "When they are doing pen testing, people can knock down pieces of infrastructure and take a system down. We can scan the network in a way that's gentle." Their focus is the security of devices (all those webcams, voice-activated assistants, and "smart" thermostats and doorbells, along with industrial equipment) connected to the internet: the Internet of Things. Servers and laptops and PCs on a network invariably have some kind of endpoint security installed: a firewall and antivirus software, at a minimum. The same could not be said of most other devices we connect to the internet. A few years earlier, there was a rash of news stories about how easily webcams could be hacked—by Peeping Toms, by child porn perverts, by nation-states. After Wong's son was born, she investigated baby monitors. "People are selling access to baby monitors on the dark web, which is super-creepy, but that's the reality," she said. Her answer was to pen-test the various products on the market. "I like the idea of looking at my baby on the phone to make sure he's okay, but I don't want anyone else to."

To drive home the importance of Suavei's mission, Wong mentioned the video doorbell that her mother had recently bought and installed in her home. The same software that allowed her mom to open the door via an app was potentially a front-door key in the hands of a clever hacker. "My mom has a Ring doorbell, but does she know how to turn on a computer? Barely," Wong said. "Think about that at scale with millions of people, tens of millions of people. People have front doors they can unlock with their phone. They can open their garage with a mobile app. People are installing these things but not managing security on them." In 2018, there were roughly seven billion devices connected to the internet. By 2022, that number is expected to swell to almost eighteen billion, according to a study they tout on the Suavei website.[*]

Wong is CEO of their company and Infante its chief technology officer. They've brought on a third person that Wong has known since before her McAfee days who is also a professor of cybersecurity at Idaho State University since selling his security intelligence company to FireEye. He's an investor in Suavei and advisor whose classes draw employees from the local water authority and energy companies who are worried about the safety of their systems. That has

---

[*] https://www.suavei.com/: "There are already 7 billion internet-connected devices in the world, and, according to Ericsson, by 2022 there will be 17.6 billion—on average, two for every human." —Alfonso Infante, CTO Suavei

prompted Suavei to add critical infrastructure as another focus area. Like lots of other security businesses, they sell products that they've built but also services, including pen testing and "preventative vulnerability management"—in English, helping a company figure out what extra security it needs to keep its most valuable data safe. Sometimes that means updating the firmware—the software programmed into a device's read-only memory. Other times it means selling an automated solution through a software-as-a-service option that has clients renting its product rather than buying the software outright.

There have been frustrations. Wong thought that one potential category of customer would be the device manufacturers but they expressed little interest in what Suavei was selling. Hiring a security firm meant acknowledging they had a problem, which could impact a company's stock price, if not also open them up to lawsuits if there were a breach. So Wong said they've switched their focus to the ISPs, who, she argued, "are the ones who really own the problem." One major carrier she had recently met with admitted that they can't identify 80 percent of the devices that are on its networks. "If you don't know what's on your network, you can't protect it," she said. In a bid to draw the ISPs as customers, Wong and her team were working on a product that would bolt basic security software to any device plugged into a participating network. Wong has also been talking to Schlumberger, the oil exploration company. "A second of downtime for them can be an economic disaster," Wong said. "We're working with them so they're able to assess their security over satellite links."

There's a downside to the entrepreneurial route. The deals she was negotiating required multiple meetings and an investment of time and effort that might never pay off if they don't land that customer. Wong was in fund-raiser mode when we met, which is never fun. They had raised $200,000 during an angel round but she estimated that they needed to secure another $1 million in investments. Such is the nature of the security business. New vulnerabilities are always being discovered. In order to survive in the business, they need to keep up with threat intelligence while also updating their product offerings and expanding the capabilities of their security appliances and services. All of this requires additional staff.

The job also entails a lot of travel, and Wong is no longer a footloose twenty-one-year-old seeking to travel the world in search of new adventures. The next month she needed to be in Australia to give a series of speeches, which meant missing her child's first Thanksgiving. She was a CEO overseeing a startup anxious to land paying customers. The speaking invites, including regional talks across the country, presented too rich an opportunity to pass up. Being a mother had long been a dream of hers but so had running her own company. "This is what I'm doing for the foreseeable future," she said. "Or maybe we'll sell the company to Symantec and the whole cycle will happen again."

That's the beauty of working in info-sec, Wong said: it's a field that largely lets you be who you want to be. She did the corporate thing for a long while, and got paid annual salaries many times that of the average American worker, and now she enjoys the freedoms born of working on her own startup. She flew around the world as a consultant when that suited her lifestyle, and more recently experienced the excitement of working incident response. If she grows bored with one job, or if her life demands a different kind of relationship with work, there's always multiple alternatives. It's like she tells students whenever she talks in front of a high school or college class: "It's hard to come up with a better career path," she said.

7

WHAT IT TAKES

Let's start with the negatives. Angela Gunn, Parisa Tabriz, and Allison Wong notwithstanding, security is still predominantly a male world. Women hold less than 20 percent of the tech jobs in the United States, "and as bad as the numbers are in tech generally, I'd say they're worse for info-sec," Gunn told me. The data bears out Gunn's instincts. As of 2018 women compromised only 11 to 14 percent of the cybersecurity workforce, according to the organization Women in Cybersecurity.[*]

"Part of me wants to scream, 'Please don't sign me up for any more women and cybersecurity efforts, I just want to get my work done,'" Gunn said. But she joins these efforts, because

---

[*] "WiCyS Announces Women in CyberSecurity 2019 Conference," Software Engineering Institute, Carnegie Mellon University, September 25, 2018, https://www.sei.cmu.edu/news-events/news/article.cfm?assetId=526358.

"if that's what it takes to get more women in here, I'll go to the meetings." But Gunn also does it her way. Feeling frustrated at a recent women-in-info-sec meeting, she blurted out, "'Can we talk about cybersecurity anytime soon?' and then watched as everyone moved away from me." By nature, she still is the journalist who struggles to understand all sides. Fewer women majoring in science, engineering, or math means a smaller pool of applicants for companies like hers. "But by God, we can do better than we're doing," she said. Pen testing in particular could use more women. "I put on a sweater, get coiffed, and I present as a harmless, middle-aged white lady," she said. "And then I'm going to own your ass." Mark Seiden said more or less the same: "If only I were a middle-aged woman pushing a food cart, I could go anywhere."

Parisa Tabriz seemed similarly ambivalent about playing ambassador for women in tech. "I don't seek to be a role model, but if other people think it's cool when they see someone like me working in tech, then that's great," she told the *Irish Times* in 2018.* In that same interview she

---

* Charlie Taylor, "Google 'Security Princess' Reigns over Web Giant's Anti-Hacking Drive," *Irish Times*, February 15, 2018, https://www .irishtimes.com/business/technology/google-security-princess-reigns- over-web-giant-s-anti-hacking-drive-1.3389586.

admitted that she had long been wary of groups that form to get more women into computer science. "I just didn't see it as the way to equality," she said.

The lack of racial diversity is another embarrassment. Consider Tabriz's employer, Google, which issues an annual diversity study reporting on its progress attaining a workplace that better reflects the wider world. Blacks account for 12 percent of the workforce in the U.S. and Latinos just less than 17 percent.[*] Yet only 2.5 percent of Google's workforce was black in 2018.[†] Only 3.6 percent of its employees were Latino. The numbers were even grimmer if we look solely at tech positions. Only 2 percent of the engineers the company hired in 2017 were African American. Slightly over 4 percent were Latino (and .3 percent Native American). By contrast, 42 percent of its tech hires in 2017 were white and 47 percent Asian (another 6

---

[*] Mark Muro, Alan Berube, and Jacob Whiton, "Black and Hispanic Underrepresentation in Tech: It's Time to Change the Equation," Brookings Institute, March 28, 2018, https://www.brookings.edu/research/black-and-hispanic-underrepresentation-in-tech-its-time-to-change-the-equation/.

[†] "Google Diversity Annual Report 2018," Google, https://static.google usercontent.com/media/diversity.google/en//static/pdf/Google_Diversity _annual_report_2018.pdf.

percent described themselves as multiracial). "The presence of blacks and Hispanics in computer and math jobs remains starkly inadequate," a trio of authors from the Brookings Institution wrote in a 2018 report.[*] Blacks account for slightly less than 8 percent of the country's computer- and math-related jobs. The gap was even larger for Latinos, who hold less than 7 percent of the country's tech jobs. Other studies have documented salary discrepancies (for women as well as people of color) and even greater underrepresentation in management and other leadership positions.[†]

---

[*] Mark Muro, Alan Berube, and Jacob Whiton, "Black and Hispanic Underrepresentation in Tech: It's Time to Change the Equation," Brookings Institute, March 28, 2018, https://www.brookings.edu/research/black-and-hispanic-underrepresentation-in-tech-its-time-to-change-the-equation/.

[†] Jason Reed and Jonathan Acosta-Rubio, "Innovation Through Inclusion: The Multicultural Cybersecurity Workforce," (ISC)2 and Frost & Sullivan, https://www.isc2.org/-/media/Files/Research/Innovation-Through-Inclusion-Report.ashx; "2017 Global Information Security Workforce Study: Women in Cybersecurity," Executive Women's Forum, https://www.ewf-usa.com/page/WomenInCybersecurity; Kathy Gurchiek, "Report: Minority Professionals in Cybersecurity Underrepresented in Senior Roles, Paid Less," Society for Human Resource Management, March 16, 2018, https://www.shrm.org/resourcesandtools/hr-topics/technology/pages/report-minority-professionals-in-cybersecurity-underrepresented-in-senior-roles-paid-less.aspx.

"You hear it all the time, 'Think like a hacker,'" Angela Gunn said. "It's basic threat modeling: put yourself in the shoes of a hacker. But I'm not Nigerian. I'm not Ukrainian. I'm not Chinese. The more people we can get into this line of work who have different backgrounds and bring a different set of experiences to the table, the better off we'll be."

Info-sec isn't for everyone. "Security can be stressful," Parisa Tabriz wrote in a 2016 post spelling out advice for strangers interested in info-sec, echoing what others had told me.[*] "It's hard to measure success with security, and in my experience, people are more likely to notice failure . . . You're dealing with ambiguous problems, imperfect solutions, limited data, and real threats to human safety." And the work is hardly like it is imagined by the popular media. "Working in security isn't like it's depicted in Hollywood," Tabriz said. "The day-to-day work isn't (in my experience) as fast-paced and sexy as it looks on screen."

"You really have to love computers," Patrick Wardle said. "This isn't something you can force. If you're not stoked on programming and figuring out computers, if you don't want

---

[*] Parisa Tabriz, "So, you want to work in security?" *Medium*, July 28, 2016, https://medium.freecodecamp.org/so-you-want-to-work-in-security-bc6c10157d23.

to be sitting inside most of the day, this career probably won't work for you."

Yet the flip side, Wardle said, is that those with an affinity for computers will find info-sec a career expansive enough to accommodate a wide range of personalities and traits. "There're a lot of people who are a little more introverted," he said. "If you're the kind who in high school was spending a lot of time on your computer or gaming, that naturally segues into a career in computers. There are jobs for people who might be on the spectrum and not super-social or outgoing. You'll still make a lot of money, you'll still love what you do for a living, but you won't have to be out there interacting with the world.

"But there's also room for people like me," Wardle continued. "I love the travel, I love to meet new people. There's that option, too." That was Allison Wong through most of her career. She was the technologist who corporations flew first-class around the globe and the corporate face when meeting with customers on behalf of McAfee and Symantec. Info-sec is big business these days, which means a slew of jobs in sales, with the need for account executives, product managers, and front-facing people who explain it all to customers and hold their hands while installing the solutions they've sold them. "Computer security is this great route because you have these extremes, from the people who sit behind a computer all day to the sales people and others out there talking to clients, traveling, always meeting people," Wardle said. "You can take one, you can take the other, or you can find some middle ground."

Is info-sec right for you? I asked everyone I spoke with that question. For Craig Williams, a director with Cisco's threat intelligence group, it boils down to desire. "For me, it was passion more than anything," said Williams, who said he knew he wanted to work with computers since first touching one in kindergarten. "When I interview people even today, I look for that. When people talk about something, you can look in their eyes and tell whether they're just regurgitating the words or actually care."

Stick-to-itiveness seems a prerequisite—a tenacity and persistence that have someone sometimes staring at a screen for fifteen straight hours. "Most of the folks I know in security, man, they just don't give up," Billy Rios said. "Just like those on the offensive don't quit, neither do we." Speaking by phone from Denver, where he now lives, Rios quoted something his wife had said at a party a couple of years back, when he had the crew of his new cybersecurity startup over for drinks. "She tells them, 'Look, here's the deal. Sometimes Billy doesn't eat. Sometimes he doesn't sleep. Don't even try to keep up with him.'" But Rios, forty, who has been in cybersecurity since leaving the Marines at twenty-four, knows plenty of the people in the info-sec world are just like him. "A lot of the folks you meet in the info-sec world are crazy-persistent," he said. "We run in the red a lot, our RPMs run high. And every once in a while, because we don't know when to quit, we get a breakthrough."

Game playing came up a lot in my interviews with people in info-sec. "There's a puzzle aspect to what we do," Parisa Tabriz said. "There's a curiosity, and also this creativity in the approach to solving the puzzle." That's applied computer science, she said: poking at the layers of abstractions and assumptions that are part of any piece of software and figuring out how to best fix (or exploit) them. Angela Gunn actually studied game theory to better understand security during her years at Hewlett-Packard as part of its Zero Day Initiative. "I tell people if they're the type who likes solving puzzles, if they like figuring out how a system works, then they'll like this work," Gunn said.

"I can teach tech skills," she continued. "I can teach you to reverse malware. But the mind-set to work your way through the puzzle is the part you can't teach." Allison Wong pretty much said the same thing. "I'm confident I can teach anybody to do cybersecurity—so long as they really have the desire and want to learn. It starts with curiosity. If you were curious and always that kid who wanted to take things apart and see how they worked, I think cybersecurity is right for you."

Craig Williams pushes the gaming comparison to the point where time-on-device in a person's formative years seems almost an early test of a person's suitability to make it in the field. "I think people underestimate how short a stepping-stone video games are to computer security," he said. Most people play by the rules and slowly get better at a game through repetition and trial and error. But Williams is interested in another type of player: the type who finds a clever way to hack the game. "Why would you play *SimCity* all day to get $1 million when you can just go change a few characters in the saved game file and get $1 million in five minutes?" he said. In this view, enlightened cheating is the highest form of gameplay. He was that type of player—and he would expect that would be true of many of the people who excel at info-sec.

"There's this security mind-set," said George Neville-

Neil, who also falls in that category of people who think
you have an instinct for info-sec or you don't. Neville-Neil
has impressive security credentials after decades in tech,
including his time with the "Paranoids" inside Yahoo. "I
wouldn't say you're born to it. But I'd say it goes click or
it doesn't." Maybe you weren't programming in the third
grade but once you started fiddling with a computer, a
recessive gene kicked in. "There's almost this instinctual
thing," he said. "If presented with something, you're
thinking, 'Hmm, how can I break this, how can I get past
this?' When presented with a problem, you're thinking of
ways around it."

Programmers, Neville-Neil continued, are generally
optimists. They need to be in order to imagine the digital
products they create. "But security people are generally
pessimists. We think everything's going to break and we're
worried about how to deal with that." Neville-Neil was one
of several people who cited an old hacker's creed: "You have
to have that hacker's attitude that information should be
free and I should be able to get a hold of it." If information
is there to be had, it must be freed and live out in the open.

Most everyone I spoke with said put down the books and
start doing. Colleges are finally teaching cybersecurity, but

how do you get the students to start thinking like black-hatted hackers? "One of the things I tell people when they're trying to get into the field is don't just read. The most important thing is to actually do it," said Charlie Miller, the "good guy" hacker who, with a partner, commandeered a Jeep Cherokee. "Try to hack stuff. Play around with your own code and look for vulnerabilities. Try to rewrite some of your stuff thinking about security." That's where he feels fortunate, Miller said. He spent five years working at the NSA after college. He was paid a salary "to sort of play around and mess with stuff and not have to worry about whether I succeeded or failed."

Parisa Tabriz is one of several people who brought up security certificates. She seemed to hold them in generally low regard. But her Google colleague, Dave Weinstein, views them as a stand-in for desire. "There's a big thing in security where people like to really hate on professional certificates," he said. "But I think they're almost right. As a signal that this person is an expert or now proficient at this? No. But they're a useful signal that someone is spending some of their time and their money because they're interested in doing security stuff. If you show me you want to get into security enough to spend your spare time and your money to go through a certificate program, then I'm interested in talking to you."

On the other hand, what's great about security is that it's also an open platform. "There are no gatekeepers," Weinstein said. "There's no main certification agency, there's no licensing like there is for a doctor or a lawyer. All you have to do is want it."

APPENDIX

As the info-sec stars who populate this book vividly demonstrate, there are any number of paths to a successful cybersecurity career, just as there are a wide range of job possibilities. Yet whatever the route taken or role played, the advice these masters provide to the wannabe ethical hacker is the same: Read. Learn. Do.

READ

Any reading list for those interested in cybersecurity begins with two seminal works. One is a short essay written by "The Mentor" (a programmer named Loyd Blankenship) and first published by the online publication *Phrack* in 1986 under the headline, "The Conscience of a Hacker." Colloquially known as the "Hacker Manifesto," it succinctly captures and explains the hacker mentality. (Sample line: "Yes, I am a criminal. My crime is that of curiosity.") The second work, written by an acclaimed programmer named Eric S. Raymond, is "How to Become a Hacker." This nine-page document celebrates hacker culture ("hackers built the internet") and what Raymond dubs the "hacker mind-set" (a quest to solve problems, a belief in open systems). Be forewarned, though: Raymond's practical advice for becoming a hacker (download and learn to use an open-source UNIX operating system, teach yourself HTML) is interspersed with more idiosyncratic suggestions (develop your appreciation of puns and wordplay, study a martial art, learn to play a musical instrument or take up singing).

The book that first exposed me—and a great number of people—to the excitement of life as an ethical hacker was *The Cuckoo's Egg*, a 1989 bestseller written by Clifford Stoll. Stoll managed the computers at Lawrence Berkeley National Laboratory, a federal research facility located in the hills above UC Berkeley. His adventure began when his boss asked him to resolve a seemingly meaningless issue: a 75-cent discrepancy in the department's ledger. That's how Stoll discovered that an unauthorized user had apparently used nine seconds of computer time but failed to pay for it. Over the next ten months, he watched as an outsider gained access to U.S. military bases whose info-sec staff had failed to change a factory default password or, worse, allowed people to log in as "guest" without even offering a password. Stoll went so far as inventing a fictitious government department within the Berkeley lab and then sweeting this made-up target by making it seem as if its people were working on a top-secret missile defense system—what today would be called a "honeypot." Ultimately, that's how Stoll caught the intruder, who turned out to be a German hacker working for the KGB.

A rogue hacker named Kevin Mitnick is the focus of the next two book recommendations: *Takedown*, which tells the story of his capture by the FBI in 1995, and *Ghost in the Wires*, the memoir he wrote after having served more than five years in prison for his crimes. "The most wanted hacker in the world," a U.S. attorney said of Mitnick in the mid-1990s—an appellation Mitnick himself would embrace years later when remaking himself as a high-priced security consultant. Mitnick was the hacker who broke into systems because he could. Yet his hacking wasn't all harmless fun. He eavesdropped on the conversations of NSA staffers because he thought it would be cool, Mitnick explained, to be "wiretapping the world's biggest wiretappers." When a woman he was interested in dating declined his advances because she was already engaged, he hacked into her financial credit report, unearthing information that broke the couple up. Mitnick married the woman but, when she sought a divorce several years later, he hacked into her voice-mail system, which is how he learned she had been having an affair with his best friend. Once he transferred $30,000 in telephone charges owed by a hospital to the home number of an acquaintance. When busted, the FBI found that he had pilfered 20,000 credit card numbers, including those belonging to some of tech's best-known figures.

Mitnick's mistake was breaking into the computer of Tsutomu Shimomura, who took the breach as a personal affront. Shimomura, a computer security expert who worked at the federally funded San Diego Supercomputer Center, is the white-hatted hero of *Takedown*, who cowrote the book with John Markoff (full disclosure: John is a former colleague of mine at the *New York Times*, and also a friend). Like *Cuckoo's Egg*, the book chronicles the pursuit and ultimate capture of an intruder who had somehow broken into a system where he had no business being. Shimomura tracked Mitnick down to an apartment outside of Raleigh, North Carolina, where the FBI arrested him. Mitnick pled guilty to various computer crimes, including illegal possession of computer files (he tricked employees at Sun Microsystems and other companies to share source code with him) and the interception of data communications (reading emails, listening in on phone conversations, and establishing network "sniffers" to grab passwords).

Ghost in the Wires is Mitnick's 2011 memoir—the entertaining autobiography of a master hacker who at the tender age of twelve had figured out how to hack the Los Angeles bus transfer system so he could ride for free. Financial gain, he pointed out, was never his motive. He never attempted to sell the corporate secrets he had obtained nor had he ever used the credit card numbers he had stolen. His exploits seemed more about showing off, if not a compulsion. "Hacking was my entertainment," Mitnick wrote. "You could almost say it was a way of escaping to an alternative reality—like playing a video game."

Parisa Tabriz suggests thinking like a hacker: Mitnick's memoir would be a good place to start your education. So would *Kingpin*, written by Kevin Poulsen. Poulson, too, spent five years in prison for computer crimes; he would reinvent himself, post-prison, as an investigative journalist. *Kingpin*, also published in 2011, is Poulson's brisk and entertaining account of the pursuit of a misfit hacker who had staged the hostile takeover of an online criminal network siphoning billions from the U.S. economy.

There are any number of other journalistic accounts to help readers better understand the dark hats that the ethical hacker must defend against. A list of the best of the genre starts with Joseph Menn's deeply reported book *Fatal System Error*. Released in 2010, Menn's book chronicles the rise of a new kind of cybercriminal: sophisticated criminal gangs that made seem quaint an internet that was once the domain of small-time thieves and those, like Mitnick, who were mainly showing off, and a new breed of cyber-sleuths struggling to keep up with them. Investigative journalist Kim Zetter turns the story of the Stuxnet worm into an engaging whodunit in her 2014 book, *Countdown to Zero Day*, and Nick Bilton, in his 2017 book, *American Kingpin*, presents a riveting tale of the mastermind behind Silk Road, a site on the Dark Web where users could buy practically anything—drugs, counterfeit money, hacking software, forged passports, poisons—free of the government's watchful eye. The Russian hacking of the 2016 U.S. presidential election has provided a rich vein for book writers. Three of the better accounts: *Russian Roulette* by Michael Isikoff and David Corn, *The Plot to Hack America* by Malcolm Nance, and *The Perfect Weapon* by David E. Sanger.

There are any number of more technical books to recommend, depending on one's area of interest. *The Hacker Playbook* by Peter Kim offers (to quote its subtitle) a "practical guide to penetration testing." Kim, a longtime security professional, includes many real-life examples while offering a step-by-step guide to pen testing. For those who, to quote Angela Gunn, "want to be that guy who opens up that malware and sees its beating heart," there are two books to read: *Practical Malware Analysis*, a step-by-step guide to dissecting malicious software by Michael Sikorski and Andrew Honig, and *Reverse Engineering for Beginners* by Dennis Yurichev.

LEARN

Take computer security classes. That could mean coursework at a two- or four-year college or returning to school for a master's degree. As mentioned in the body of the book, more and more universities are offering undergraduate and advanced degrees in computer security. These days any number of well-regarded schools offer an online master's in some element of info-sec.[*] Earn an online master's in criminal justice with a concentration in cybercrime investigation and cybersecurity at Boston University, for instance, or a master's in cybersecurity policy and management at Arizona State University. Champlain College in Vermont offers a pair of advanced online cybersecurity degrees: one in information security operations and another in digital forensics.

[*] "Top 25 Schools with Online Master's in Cyber Security Programs for 2019," Cyber Degrees, https://www.cyberdegrees.org/listings/top-online-masters-in-cyber-security-programs/.

The University at California at Berkeley offers an online master of information and cybersecurity.

A less expensive, less time-intensive option is the plethora of webinars and online videos that provide primers on different aspects of security. One great alternative is the Cybrary,[*] which offers free cyber-training classes on a wide range of topics, including pen testing, cybercrime forensics, and auditing a system to test for vulnerabilities.

Learning also entails keeping current on the latest threats. Regularly visit news sites such as *Motherboard* (its slogan, "The future is wonderful, the future is terrifying"[†]) and *Ars Technica*,[‡] both of which do a terrific job covering the latest security flaws and breaches. Read "Krebs on Security,"[§] a news-driven blog written by former *Washington Post* reporter Brian Krebs, and *Hackers News*,[¶] a social news website run by Y Combinator, a Silicon Valley–based investment fund and startup incubator. Parisa Tabriz suggested three sites that let

---

[*] https://www.cybrary.it/

[†] https://motherboard.vice.com/en_us/page/about=motherboard

[‡] https://arstechnica.com/

[§] https://krebsonsecurity.com

[¶] https://news.ycombinator.com/

those interested follow the exploits of some of the more high-profile bug hunters and learn from their triumphs: Bugtraq[*], Full-Disclosure, and OSS-Sec.[†] Visit bugcrowd,[‡] which maintains a public bug bounty list. Use Twitter to follow top security researchers such as Patrick Wardle and Charlie Miller for their twist on the latest news. Others to follow include Katie Moussouris ("@k8emO"), a high-profile bug bounty hunter, and Jake Williams ("@MalewareJake"), an ex-NSA'er and active security researcher.

DO

And, finally, do. Get yourself to Las Vegas for the Black Hat and DEF CON conferences held there each summer. Both are essential networking events that include talks from some of the field's top talent and breakout sessions on a range of topics. Attend some of the other security conferences mentioned in the book and find out what's going on in your area. Cities around the country hold annual Security BSides conferences,[§] which are

---

* http://bugtraq-team.com/

† https://seclists.org/oss-sec/

‡ https://www.bugcrowd.com/bug-bounty-list/

§ http://www.securitybsides.com/w/page/12194156/FrontPage

aimed at community building and fostering conversations about computer security. Listen to the talks and see what sparks your interest. Seek out Meetup groups in your area and join industry groups. Learn from practitioners and, if possible, interact with them. Is security right for you? If so, what role might be the best fit for you? There's no better way of exploring those questions than talking to people in the field. It's part of the process: one generation of info-sec helps the next, just as they invariably had been given a hand early in their careers.

"Check other out career fairs and conferences," Parisa Tabriz counseled. "Get involved in clubs or organizations. Apply for internships and part-time jobs with bold enthusiasm."

And, finally, takes those first steps toward thinking like a hacker. Remember what Mark Seiden said: it's much harder to find ways of breaking into a program if you've never created one. Write a program and then try to beat your own program. And spend time in what Tabriz called "hacker playgrounds." Hack This Site[*] is a safe and free site that she used to test herself and expand her skills while still in college. Graduate to a self-guided hacker training site such as Infosec Rocks[†] and then the real

---

[*] https://www.hackthissite.org/

[†] https://sites.google.com/site/infosecrocks/

world of using debuggers and network scanners and software fuzz testing.

"Find and report bugs in actual software you use," Tabriz suggested. Any number of software vendors offer cash rewards for exploitable bugs. Or try fixing bugs in an open-source project. Many open-source projects rely on people to serve as its beta testers who can find and fix problems. "The project will thank you, and it's typically a good way to get real-world experience and your foot in the door for future work," Tabriz said.

And the feeling of that first hack, many of the people quoted within these pages can tell you, is all they ever needed to know computer security was the right choice for them.

ACKNOWLEDGMENTS

First and foremost, thanks to Angela Gunn, Mark Seiden, Parisa Tabriz, Patrick Wardle, Dave Weinstein, and Allison Wong for letting me into their lives and sharing their stories. Without them, there would be no book. I'm thankful, too, for the others who were similarly forthcoming about their lives, many of whom are quoted within these pages. I only wish I could have included everyone's stories. Each was more interesting than the next.

Jonathan Karp, the president and publisher of Simon & Schuster, has long been a great supporter of my book-writing habit. And for that I'm eternally grateful. I'm thankful Ben Loehnen invited me to take part in the Masters at Work series, which struck me as a great idea from the moment I heard it, and I'm lucky to have worked with the talented Stuart Roberts, who helped me shape the final narrative and cut away the excesses. Big thanks as well to Jonathan Evans and Dominick Montalto, for the care with which they copyedited this book and gave it a final sanding.

An author couldn't be luckier in his choice of agents, Elizabeth Kaplan, who is always there with sage advice and her friendship. Thanks, Elizabeth. And thanks as well to two friends who agreed to take the time to read this manuscript. Both make brief cameos in the book. One, Dan Goodin, is the tech journalist offered a job in security while in the waiting area of a San Francisco restaurant and also a security reporter for Ars Technica, a must-read publication for anyone getting into info-sec. The other, Mike Kelly, worked at Microsoft in the 1990s into the early 2000s and saw the changes in attitudes there (and industrywide) toward security and its importance. Thanks both for your corrections and maybe even saving me from myself.

And of course there's Daisy, Oliver, and Silas. Talk about lucky. Daisy always urges me forward toward what's worth doing, and Oliver and Silas keep a smile on our faces. And maybe my sons were even a bit impressed with me now that they could tell their friends at school that their old man was spending time with some of the coolest hackers on the planet.

ABOUT THE AUTHOR

GARY RIVLIN is a Pulitzer Prize–winning investigative reporter and the author of five books, including *Katrina: After the Flood*. His work has appeared in *The New York Times Magazine*, *Mother Jones*, *GQ*, and *Wired*, among other publications. He is a two-time Gerald Loeb Award winner and former reporter for the *New York Times*. He lives in New York with his wife, theater director Daisy Walker, and two sons.